PREACH THE WORD

The Bible Study Textbook Series

NEW TESTAMENT

The Bible Study New Testament Ed. By Rhoderick Ice	**The Gospel of Matthew** In Four Volumes By Harold Fowler (Vol. IV not yet available)	**The Gospel of Mark** By B. W. Johnson and Don DeWelt
The Gospel of Luke By T. R. Applebury	**The Gospel of John** By Paul T. Butler	**Acts Made Actual** By Don DeWelt
Romans Realized By Don DeWelt	**Studies in Corinthians** By T. R. Applebury	**Guidance From Galatians** By Don Earl Boatman
The Glorious Church (Ephesians) By Wilbur Fields	**Philippians - Colossians Philemon** By Wilbur Fields	**Thinking Through Thessalonians** By Wilbur Fields
Paul's Letters To Timothy & Titus By Don DeWelt	**Helps From Hebrews** By Don Earl Boatman	**James & Jude** By Don Fream
Letters From Peter By Bruce Oberst	**Hereby We Know (I-II-III John)** By Clinton Gill	**The Seer, The Saviour, and The Saved (Revelation)** By James Strauss

OLD TESTAMENT

O.T. History By William Smith and Wilbur Fields	**Genesis** In Four Volumes By C. C. Crawford	**Exploring Exodus** By Wilbur Fields	**Leviticus** By Don DeWelt
Numbers By Brant Lee Doty	**Deuteronomy** By Bruce Oberst	**Joshua - Judges Ruth** By W. W. Winter	**I & II Samuel** By W. W. Winter
I & II Kings By James E. Smith	**I & II Chronicles** By Robert E. Black	**Ezra, Nehemiah & Esther** By Ruben Ratzlaff & Paul T. Butler	**The Shattering of Silence (Job)** By James Strauss
Psalms In Two Volumes By J. B. Rotherham		**Proverbs** By Donald Hunt	**Ecclesiastes and Song of Solomon** — By R. J. Kidwell and Don DeWelt
Isaiah In Three Volumes By Paul T. Butler		**Jeremiah and Lamentations** By James E. Smith	**Ezekiel** By James E. Smith
Daniel By Paul T. Butler		**Hosea - Joel - Amos Obadiah - Jonah** By Paul T. Butler	**Micah - Nahum - Habakkuk Zephaniah - Haggai - Zechariah Malachi** — By Clinton Gill

SPECIAL STUDIES

The Church In The Bible By Don DeWelt	**The Eternal Spirit** By C. C. Crawford	**World & Literature of the Old Testament** Ed. By John Willis	**Survey Course In Christian Doctrine** Two Bks. of Four Vols. By C. C. Crawford
New Testament History — Acts By Gareth Reese	**Learning From Jesus** By Seth Wilson		**You Can Understand The Bible** By Grayson H. Ensign

PREACH THE WORD

Guidelines to Expository Preaching

By

Charles R. Gresham

College Press Publishing Company, Joplin, Missouri

Library of Congress Catalog Card Number: 83-71917
International Standard Book Number: 0-89900-198-X

TABLE OF CONTENTS

CONTRIBUTORS

PREFACE

This volume, *Preach The Word*, has been produced for one basic reason, and that is to lift up the importance of Expository Preaching within the Church of the twentieth century. Preaching, generally, has fallen upon "evil days"; Expository Preaching, particularly, is in decline. Too often, what preaching is done is topical, moralistic, sensational and uses Scripture only for embellishment or as prooftexts for some already preconceived theme. This ought not to be!

We are attempting to "beam" this volume to young "preachers in preparation." We hope this volume will have wide circulation in Christian Colleges and Seminaries; for it is here that patterns are developed and set which will be continued throughout years of specialized ministry. The volume is dedicated to that rising group of young preachers with the anticipation that they will find in it some motivation toward a pulpit ministry that is truly expositional with reference to the sacred text.

The pattern of this volume is apparent. Following two introductory essays which attempt to define Expository Preaching and set it in the context of the Restoration Movement, there are two major divisions. The first is a series of essays by some of the outstanding preachers within Christian Churches and Churches of Christ indicating some of those features and factors that they find important in their preparation for preaching. The second division is a series of expository sermons by the same men who have indicated how they go about their preparation. Thus, the results of their preparation will be seen.

We have not tried to seek any uniformity, either in the sermons or in the essays explicating processes of preparation. Some of the sermons are in more outline form, others are developed into a full manuscript. Some of the essays are brief, others more extended. We believe that such diversity and lack of uniformity in themselves are significant teaching aids. No two preachers preach alike or prepare alike. By opening the study doors of these diverse Christian men and listening to the variety of their preaching, we can understand how God does use all of us as vessels of his redeeming and graceful water of life.

There is also a special sermon on "our Plea" which is not strictly expositional. However, this sermon indicates a way to respond to an ever-present need—the need to keep before our people the heritage that we have and to see this in terms of certain current trends.

We have also included a Contributors section in the book. We believe that a certain amount of biographical data will enhance both the preparation essays and the sermons. This section reveals the diversity mentioned above, both in past academic preparation and present ministry. You will note that these men are in varying ministerial roles—college presidents, campus ministries, professors, editors, as well as local church ministers. The one common characteristic that unites them (as far as this volume is concerned) is that they are all excellent biblical preachers.

We send forth this volume with the prayer that it will encourage "great" preaching. Great preaching occurs, not when the man is foremost, but when the Lord of that man is revealed through adequate exposition of Scriptural truth.

C. R. Gresham

WHAT IS EXPOSITORY PREACHING?

By Edwin V. Hayden

I love expository preaching. I thoroughly enjoy hearing an expository sermon; and when I preach I seldom use any other kind. If I can believe what I read and hear from teachers of homiletics, my high regard for expository preaching is generally shared among the craft. And that has its disadvantages.

You see, if all the teachers and critics of sermonizing spread a convincing rumor that expository preaching is the best kind of preaching, some adjustments will have to be made. Either a lot of preachers will have to change their sermonizing habits, or they will have to formulate a definition of "expository preaching" so as to make it include what they are doing. The alternative is to admit frankly that they are coming up with something less than the best, and that would be devastating to the ministerial ego. Personally, I should much prefer to hear them stand up and argue the superiority of their own brand of sermonizing, rather than to indulge in adjusted definitions, changing labels on the product.

Actually, expository preaching may not always and everywhere be the best kind for every preacher. But I'm convinced that it is best for me, wherever I have been, as speaker or hearer. It offers some peculiar advantages that cannot be enjoyed without developing the peculiar qualities of expository sermonizing.

General definition—I have developed my own definition of expository preaching, which seems in harmony with the classic definitions given in homiletical texts. An expository sermon is, I think, one that *begins with a substantial passage of Scripture* and *allows the principal thoughts of*

1

that passage to become the outline for development and the basis for application.

The "substantial passage" of Scripture is typically a paragraph of six to a dozen verses; but it may be a chapter, a book, a biography drawn from several passages, or a group of closely related passages from more than one book —as in the case of certain Psalms related either to Old Testament history or to a passage from the Gospels. The "substantial passage," on the other hand, may possibly be as brief as a verse, in which case the sermon would be very close to a textual sermon, but deriving its expository quality from amplification built on related passages.

The "principal thoughts" that provide the sermon outline may or may not be found in the exact words of any one translation. In fact, before building on specific words and phrases, the preacher should examine the passage carefully in the original language if possible, but certainly in several different translations. Otherwise he may be tempted to place too much weight on the wrong corner of the word in question. The "appearance of evil" (1 Thessalonians 5:22), for example, is not the semblance of evil in what is innocent within itself; it is rather the emergence of evil wherever, whenever, and in whatever guise it may show itself. The apostle's advice is to stay far from evil wherever it sticks up its head. This becomes clear in the various translations.

The "principal thoughts" also lead the preacher to a *sermon*, rather than to a commentary or even to a lecture. This becomes the more evident as he deals with larger blocks of Scripture. Obviously he cannot say in one sermon all that can, or should, or must be said on the basis of a whole book, or a chapter, or even a long paragraph. But

2

as in surveying a mountain range, he may view the contours of the whole, while giving attention to the highest peaks. Later he may come back for another view of the same range from the other side, or in reference to other of its peaks, or even its notable passes and canyons. So the expository preacher will almost never exhaust his text in one sermon. He will usually find that any attempt to do so will exhaust only himself and his hearers.

Translating principal thoughts into outline is an exercise worthy of ceaseless attention, boundless imagination, and relentless practice. Yet the veriest novice need not despair. He can expound plainly what the Scripture plainly says, to the profit both of himself and those that hear him. On the other hand, the veteran's utmost skill will find a worthy challenge in discovering symmetry, beauty, and dramatic force in the text, without going beyond the warrant of "thus saith the Lord." He will gain attention, memory, and response for his efforts.

How many divisions will an expository sermon have? How many peaks stand out on this side of the mountain range? It may be anywhere from two to a dozen, with three or four probably to be preferred for hearing, recalling, and responding.

The realm of application and exhortation distinguishes the sermon from the lecture. Something in each of those grand thoughts of Scripture stirs the preacher—and through him stirs his hearers—to love God more fervently and to serve Him more fully because they have examined it together.

The application involves change. Another word for the same thing is *repentance*. The hearer will be and do something different because he heard that sermon than otherwise he would have been and would have done.

3

Reproof and rebuke are legitimate parts of sermon application. They should come from what God says in the text rather than from what the preacher thinks about current events and congregational appearances. (What, incidentally, *is* the source of all that scolding we endure for wearing a sober countenance in the house of the Lord?) God's reproofs must be conveyed, of course, with God's love and God's fervor. And they must be accompanied with that other kind of sermonic application—encouragement, exhortation, and strengthening of faith.

Varieties of treatment—The grand texts of God's Word have offered themselves for my preaching pleasure under a wide variety of developments—all expository under the general definition just presented.

Most common and natural is the *paragraph* or *chapter* that breaks down into consecutive parts, as, for example, Mark 7:31-37 for a reminder that "Jesus Does All Things Well." It falls into two unequal parts: (1) Jesus Did, and (2) The People Did. Jesus met a man's need: (a) where He found it; (b) with understanding (that a deaf mute was probably sensitive and would be embarrassed by a public display in healing); (c) with considerate kindness (that not only refused to embarrass the man but made him an understanding participant in the healing); and (d) with adequate power. On the other hand the people (a) admired Jesus, but (b) disobeyed Him.

The third chapter of James offers itself for a sermon to preachers and prospective preachers under the title, "Occupational Hazards": (1) The Weight of Responsibility—vv. 1, 2 (2) The Way of Words—vv. 2-12; and (3) The Wisdom of the World—vv. 13-18.

Luke 5:1-11 affords opportunity to view both sides of recruitment for service. It calls for two sermons, one examining what Jesus found in Simon Peter, "The Kind of Workman God Can Use"; and the other reflecting on what Simon saw in Jesus, "The Kind of Employer You Are Looking For." Tracing the story from the coming of Jesus followed by the multitude along Galilee's shore, to the fishermen's abandonment of their boats to accept full-time discipleship towards fishing for men, we discover these elements. The acceptable *workman* is reflected in an acrostic outline: W orking (v. 5), O rderly (v. 2), R espectful (v. 3), K nowing the Lord (v. 5), M eek (v. 8), A ble to choose the best in preference to the good (v. 11), and N ow-conscious (v. 11). The supremely worthy employer may have been discovered in the same events to be Respected (v. 1), Responsive and Resourceful (vv. 3, 4, 6), Receptive of His colleagues' contributions (vv. 3, 4), Relevant to the real needs of men (vv. 1, 3), Reliable even in the most incredible circumstances (vv. 5-7), Rewarding (vv. 5-7), Regardful of His associates (v. 10), and Requiring of their full capacities (vv. 10, 11). One passage, two sermons, both expository and both practical.

John 3:1-21 and John 4:5-42, on the other hand, invite the weaving of *two passages into one sermon,* tracing the importance of informal personal conversations, "Just Between Us Two." We may observe the contrasts between the two interviews; night and noonday, Jerusalem and Samaria, honored ruler and wastrel woman. This serves only to emphasize the elements in which the conversations were alike, beginning with the same respect for the conversant as a person, and the same concern for the conversant's need of God; picking up with queries and observations

5

based on the immediate circumstances and evident interests; pressing to the need for, and the presence of Messiah; and eventuating in a clear declaration of the truth that has been called the Golden text of the Bible! After this, how dare any Christian consider private conversation trivial, to be wasted in small talk, or worse?

The text is *not always* treated *in consecutive order.* A sermon from Matthew 8, on the "Power and Authority of Christ," builds on Matthew 7:28, 29, with its notice concerning Jesus' authority, and recognizes a practical difference between His exercise of sheer *power over things* and His *authority over people.* We observe His power over sickness—leprosy (8:2-4), disease at a distance (8:5-13), and the illness so suddenly healed that the patient started waiting on the family (8:14, 15); His power over the natural world of wind and sea (8:23-27); and His total, unresisted power over demons (8:28-32). This last event provides an amazing transition, as we see the all-powerful Lord suddenly yielding to the Gadarene citizens' demand that He depart from their shores (8:34—9:1). So we go back to the heart of Matthew 8 to observe that Jesus' authority over people, unlike His power over things, is accepted voluntarily or not at all (8:19, 20); but if accepted it must be absolute (8:21, 22). Yet the purpose of all this power and authority, far from being His own glorification, is rather to relieve *our* weaknesses and to bear *our* afflictions (8:16, 17). In this treatment we have scrambled the order of the chapter a bit, but I think we have preserved its message.

The main thoughts of a Scripture passage *cannot always be distinguished in separate paragraphs, verses, or phrases.* Sometimes, like the various colors in a block of marble, the grand themes twine themselves throughout the piece. Such a passage is Romans 6:1-13, evidently designed to employ the Christians' baptistmal experience to remind them of something they had forgotten about Christian living. The sermon here is "A Matter of Death and Life," to be contrasted with life-and-death concerns in which desperately fearful folk cling to life with slipping fingers and think of death as having the last word. No! In Christ, death is the way-station and life the triumphant finale. It is death and life, in that order! The passage may be pressented in three divisions: (1) Christ is dead and alive for our sakes; (2) We are dead and alive for Christ's sake; and (3) The bond between His experience and ours is found in Christian baptism.

The "plan of salvation" can be traced with fascinating interest through *expository treatment of conversion stories* in the book of Acts. There is rich variety in the circumstances and personalities; but the solid core—hearing of Christ, believing Christ, repentance toward Christ, confession of Christ, baptism into Christ, and life in Christ— runs unmistakably through them all. In most instances the prospective converts might have seemed not to need converting, but converted they were, through the Spirit-led preaching of the apostles. Acts 9:1-19; 22:3-16; 26:9-20 recounts "The Conversion of a Religious Man." Acts 10:1— 11:14 relates "The Conversion of a Righteous Man." Acts 8:26-39 tells "The Conversion of a Thoughtful Man" (he was reading the Scriptures on his month-long trip home from church!). Acts 16:16-34 records "The Conversion of an Active Man." (He was so little given to thoughtful investigation that he would have taken his own life without even looking beyond an open door for evidence of the

7

reason. If Paul's first response to him had mentioned baptism, he would have been baptized before hearing, and would never have learned why!)

Acts 10:1—11:14, viewed from another angle, provides the *expository background for a single-verse text* (10:33) answering a preacher's query to his audience: "Why Did You Send for Me?" Cornelius' statement provides the framework for discussion of the whole incident: (1) We Are All Here Present (who, and how assembled—vv. 2, 24, 27); (2) Before God—vv. 2, 30, etc.; (3) To Hear— 10:5, 22; 11:14; (4) All Things That Are Commanded Thee of God (a remarkably inclusive and exclusive assignment, leading to consideration of what Peter did say on that occasion). Give almost any preacher that kind of spirit, expectation, and demand in his audience, and you are likely to get great preaching!

From Text to Sermon—For me, the text grows into a sermon by a rather simple, threefold process: *Reconstruct, Compare,* and *Apply.* It's a convenient RCA for communication.

Putting the process to work is much less simple. Each step involves much that has been learned from books of homiletics and perhaps even more that has been learned from exercise at the art. But the process can be used helpfully, I think, at any level of experience. The steps are useful for walking as well as for running.

A good deal of curiosity goes into *reconstructing* the biblical incident. It includes all the common questions beginning with W: Who said it? To Whom? When? Where? Why? Under what circumstances?

Most important is the question that should be most obvious: What exactly did the writer/speaker say? The recorders and translators of Scripture have done marvelously well at bringing God's Word to us in human words; but our end of the communication is helped considerably by inquiring into the text in the original languages and various translations.

Reconstruction can be tremendously exciting, as in measuring the words of Luke 5:5—a lifelong fisherman's response to a Carpenter's ridiculous directive concerning fishing! And I'll not soon forget discovering in Israel that seventeen-year-old Joseph, having been sold to the traders at Dothan (Genesis 37:12-28) actually traveled for at least two days *toward,* and then *past* his home at Hebron as he was taken in slavery to Egypt.

Sometimes the reconstruction can be vitally important, as in tracing the meanings of *repent* and *baptize.* Sometimes it does no more than add interest and excitement to the message, for the preacher and his audience. But even then it is a rewarding experience.

Comparing interweaves with, and builds upon, reconstruction. The comparison deals with persons, places, texts, teachings, applications, and probably much more. Where else and under what other circumstances do we meet the persons involved in our text? To what persons of our present or historic acquaintance can they be likened? What else happened at the place described? How long would it have taken the characters in the story to go from this place to another? Where else does the Bible say something like what it says here? Where does it say something significantly different? How do the instructions given in this text compare with what are given elsewhere and under other circumstances? Note, for example, that Jesus took a deaf mute "aside from the multitude" (Mark 7:33) to

9

heal him; whereas He directed that blind Bartimaeus should be brought to Him at the center of attention (Luke 18:39, 40). Did you ever wonder why?

Perhaps the most important comparisons deal with *application*. In what ways are we, now, like those folk, then? How, then, do their experiences rest with us as examples, and how do the instructions given to them obligate us to obedience?

Without vital application a message is not a sermon, and speaking is not preaching. The apostles made it abundantly clear that God's revelation in Christ laid an unavoidable obligation on their hearers. It is so also with us. That obligation, in its manifold aspects and expressions, is in the end and aim of all preaching.

The preaching needs to be careful and responsible, however, in each step of sermon construction. Like the builder of a house, he must know the difference between framework and ornamentation, or between bearing walls and movable partitions. Experience, reason, and creative imagination are among the preacher's necessary tools in each step of sermon building, just as glass, paint, and fabric are necessary to the completion of an attractive dwelling; but you don't build on them! Let experience, reason, and imagination provide the decoration that adds interest and attractiveness to the sermon; but never rest on experience, reason, or imagination for argument, teaching, or essential applications. Let the weight of all these structural elements rest squarely on a clear "thus saith the Lord!" To do otherwise is to build for ultimate collapse; it is to preach divisive doctrines; it is to raise a foolish challenge against the sole authority of God's Son. Preach the Word!

A Preaching Program—Up to this point we have dealt not so much with expository *preaching* as with expository *sermons*. And there is a difference. I preach expository sermons when I am invited to fill pulpits or to speak on convention programs. In each case I measure the assignment and the circumstance, and I seek a passage of Scripture that fills the need. From that passage I speak. But in each case this is one-time sermonizing. I could do the same sort of one-time sermonizing from selected passages in the same pulpit twice every Sunday for ten years, and not engage fully in expository *preaching*. *Expository preaching* demands a continuing, consistent linkage with the Word of God.

The heart of expository preaching is the gospel itself— the story of Jesus. The climactic events of the gospel are summarized in the first four verses of 1 Corinthians 15: "That Christ died for our sins according to the scriptures; and that he was buried, and that he rose again the third day according to the scriptures." But these four verses cannot fully acquaint us with Him who died for our sins; nor show how His ministry fulfilled the Scriptures; nor inform us concerning the nature of His death; nor reveal the Sonship of Him whom God raised from the dead. To meet these needs the Holy Spirit has provided us with not four verses, but four books—the first four books in the volume we call the New Testament. And those four comprise almost half the total bulk of the entire volume. New Testament preachers ought to accept the proportionate suggestion!

Evangelism—the preaching of the evangel—does not end with the experience of baptism into Christ. In fact, the apostle Paul used that very experience of baptism as a starting point for evangelizing the Roman Christians (Romans 6:1-13). His sermon on Christian living was a sermon about Jesus, with application in the Christian's relationship to His death and resurrection. Likewise Paul's sermon on humility, written to the Christians at Philippi, was a review of the gospel, evangelizing those fine, faithful, and generous brethren in Macedonia (Philippians 2:1-11).

The entire book of Luke was, in fact, written to a man (or a people) who had been instructed in the gospel and needed an orderly, authoritative review of it to establish the certainty of the facts already accepted (Luke 1:1-4). Luke was evangelizing Christians!

Expository preaching, then, must by its very nature give major time and emphasis to the Scriptures concerning Jesus —not simply the Easter-week events of Jerusalem's northern environs, but the lifelong self-giving that took place from Galilee to Judea, with expansions into Syrophenicia and Egypt.

Building around the gospel, expository preaching needs to give orderly attention to the entire Bible. My own need as a preacher, and what seemed to be the needs of the people to whom I preached, led me long ago to adopt a peculiarly satisfying "Bible Book of the Month" program for congregational reading and expository preaching. Briefly, it entailed choosing for each month a book, or a group of shorter books, to be read by the people and to be preached from the pulpit. The reading gained interest from the preaching, and the preaching gained force from the reading. We dealt alternately with Old Testament books (giving New Testament application) and New Testament materials. The Gospels were scheduled for attention at frequent intervals. Each month we distributed introductory leaflets, providing a survey and outline of the book(s) chosen, and the topics and texts for sermons during that month.

The program answered a real need in the preacher. It provided a bulwark against "hobby" preaching, and against the neglect of large areas of revealed truth. It helped greatly in the approach to sensitive subjects and sensitive folk. Each sermon came in order from the materials being read by the entire church; and no accusation of personal attack could be established. As a whole, the program rested in the divine wisdom that provided the Bible. As such it met needs in the congregation that were unknown to the preacher, and it supplied preventive teaching, so as to cure some ills before they developed.

At the same time the program allowed for considerable freedom in choosing texts and topics for special days, special occasions, and special needs. Scriptural guidance and limitation balanced nicely with personal freedom and responsibility in the choosing of sermon material covering perhaps half a dozen chapters each month out of the material (ranging from fifteen to fifty chapters, with an average of about thirty) being read by the congregation.

The program responded to a need in the church. It encouraged Bible reading. Not all the people responded, but many did, and the level of Bible reading increased. A chapter a day is no great involvement in Bible study, but it is much better than nothing.

Perhaps the greatest value for the people lay in the two-way relation and mutual reinforcement between their own reading and the pulpit preaching. Both aspects of their Christian experience were enriched.

13

As the program unfolded it provided a way to see the whole Bible in proportion, and to recognize its parts in relation one to another. And it said plainly to all who knew of the plan, "This congregation is a people of the Book!"

Do you see now why I love expository preaching—which is at least one long step ahead of expository sermonizing? I hope you'll come to love it, too.

PREACHING IN THE RESTORATION MOVEMENT

By C. R. Gresham

The principals and practices of preaching as set out in the Restoration Movement have been quite varied. In the early "Christian" movements of James O'Kelly and Barton W. Stone preaching was linked with a system of revivalism and was done within a context of hyper-emotionalism. Stone and his followers had broken with strict Calvinism, in which preaching could be seen only as warning, seldom as promise. They were emphasizing the saving work of Christ as the central content of preaching. Their style, however, was the typical approach on the frontier in which the preaching was designed to induce certain emotional responses which would be accepted as the outpouring of the Spirit and, therefore, evidence of pardon. One sees this approach reflected in Brother Stone's and David Purviance's autobiographies and in the works of John and Samuel Rogers, who were prominent leaders among the "Christians" of the West.

When Alexander Campbell came upon the scene, he was to give special attention to both the content and style of preaching. This grew out of his reaction to the "clergy system" which he believed was detrimental to the Christian movement. Not only did Campbell write scathing strictures on the preaching as evidenced in his day (one sees this primarily in his journal, *The Christian Baptist,* where he feels he must be more negative and iconoclastic), but demonstrations of this concern are also seen in his later writings and in the more irenic *Millennial Harbinger,* which he edited from 1830 to 1866.

In Campbell, preaching is integrally linked with sound hermeneutics. Since preaching is the proclamation of God's

15

truth revealed, it is necessary for the preacher to give himself to a proper understanding of the whole counsel of God revealed in Scripture, making those dispensational and covenantal distinctions that are clearly seen in Scripture. Campbell's famous *Sermon on the Law* (1816) was an example of this hermeneutical concern and precipitated clerical opposition because most preachers of that day were what Campbell called "scrap doctors." By this he meant taking phrases of the Bible here and there, relating them to each other, and making them say what they do not say, understood contextually, or dispensationally.

Campbell, by nature, was not highly emotional. He was not a product of the frontier as were O'Kelly, Stone, Purviance and others. Therefore, he did not look with favor upon the hyper-emotionalism of revivalism. His concept of faith as belief in the testimony of credible witnesses was coupled with a type of preaching and teaching that was designed to elicit such faith, not to trigger some emotional response.

Walter Scott's recovery of the ancient pattern of New Testament evangelism (what he called "The Gospel Restored"), in which preaching is seen as the proclamation of the Gospel centering in the Messiahship of Jesus, accompanied by an invitation similar to that of Peter in Acts 2, is an added facet to the Campbellian approach in preaching. Pardon is now evidenced by willingness to believe the testimony concerning Christ's Saviorhood to repent and to be immersed into Christ, at which time remission of sins and the gift of the Holy Spirit are guaranteed by a gracious Heavenly Father (this invitation was often known as Scott's "five-finger exercise").

From 1828 on (the year in which Scott came to promote this "Ancient Gospel" on the Western Reserve), the Campbell movement (and, later, the bulk of the merged Campbell-Stone movement) began to make a clear distinction between preaching and teaching. What C. H. Dodd would popularize in our century in his *The Apostolic Preaching and Its Development* was clearly set out by Scott (*The Gospel Restored*), Campbell, and other secondary leaders (e.g. B. A. Hinsdale, *Jesus as Teacher* [1895]). Preaching is the proclamation of the facts of the Gospel, leading one to salvation; teaching is the continued instruction of those who are now Christian in all the implications of the Gospel, the truths of the Christian system, and the ethical responses demanded by the Lordship of Christ.

We are indebted to W. T. Moore for understanding something of the later trends in Restoration preaching. Both in 1868 and in 1918, fifty years later, he edited volumes of representative sermons by leading preachers of the Restoration Movement. The 1868 volume (*The Living Pulpit of the Christian Church*) included 28 sermonic discourses by leading preachers and educators of that day. These sermons are "thematic," that is, they are expositions of great biblical truths and principles. They follow Campbell's approach in emphasizing sound hermeneutics and revealing the whole counsel of God. They are Christocentric, however, reflecting what was the heart of the Restoration ideal—the simple creed of "Christians only."

The 1918 volume (*The New Living Pulpit of the Christian Church*) is of a different caliber. Though it includes sermons from ostensible leading preachers and teachers of the progressive wing of the Restoration Movement of that time, there is not the uniformity of "thematic," biblical preaching, as in the 1868 volume. Most of these sermons are topical (some even trivially topical!). There are a few sermons that are thematic, a few that are "expository," in the sense that that term is used presently, but most are topical and several are noted for their absence of biblical material. Several sermons reflect problems of that period, showing that preaching, particularly among the more liberal, was becoming more issue-centered. This volume also shows (in contrast to that 1868 volume) that sermonizing was becoming more an art. Several of the sermons reflect high oratorical skill and artistry. Whereas the sermons in the earlier volume were more intellectual and educational, in 1918 the sermons are more inspirational and persuasive. Method has become more important; communication must now break through more barriers.

The varied pattern of *The New Living Pulpit of the Christian Church* continues to be evidenced in current preaching. Within the three major wings of the Movement, a variety of preaching is apparent. In the more conservative Churches of Christ, there is still a thematic approach evidenced, though too often, in a rather rigid, legalistic manner with little or no depth in true biblical understanding. Yet in this same segment there are outstanding biblical expository and thematic preachers. Among the Christian Churches and Churches of Christ, variety is seen as well. Many of these preachers tend toward topical preaching, little different (except in sophistication) from that to which Campbell reacted in the nineteenth century. Yet, here there is great thematic and expository preaching as well and teachers of Homiletics in the Bible college are stressing biblical preaching. The Christian Church (Disciples of Christ), tends to manifest preaching that is more issue-oriented, therefore, less biblical and more topical. Yet, within this group examples of a biblically-informed expository ministry will also be found.

In all three segments, preaching is still highly important, and, along with the Lord's Supper, is central to the liturgy of worship. Though not often seen among the more liberal churches in The Christian Church (Disciples of Christ), preaching in "revivals" or "evangelistic meetings" ("Gospel meetings" is the favorite term among the conservative "Churches of Christ") is still emphasized in the other two segments of the Movement.

FOR ADDITIONAL READING

Fitch, Alger Morton, Jr. *Alexander Campbell, Preacher of Reform and Reformer of Preaching*. Austin, TX: Sweet Publishing Co., 1970.

Moore, W. T. "Introduction" (an excellent survey of the History of Preaching, both generally and within the early Restoration Movement), *The New Living Pulpit of the Christian Church*. St. Louis: Christian Board of Publication, 1918.

Stevenson, Dwight E. *Disciple Preaching in the First Generation, An Ecological Study*. Nashville, TN: The Disciples of Christ Historical Society, 1969.

Walker, Granville T. Preaching in the Thought of Alexander Campbell. St. Louis: Bethany Press, 1954.

PREPARATION OF
AN EXPOSITORY SERMON

By Knofel Staton

Introduction. I consider two cautions to be extremely important in the preparation of expository sermons. These are necessary to allow the individual preacher freedom for variety of expression. The first caution is: Do not get trapped into just one type of expository sermon. An expository sermon may be the exposition of a word or phrase study, the exposition of a short section of Scripture, the exposition of a long section of Scripture, or the exposition of an entire book of the Bible. Edification of the membership calls for the usage of each of these types.

The second caution is: Do not get trapped into just one form of exposition. The text and the intention of the preacher should dictate the form. Some texts lend themselves naturally to an outline with three points, but others do not. If the outline does not communicate the meaning of the text in its literary context, it is a forced outline. Of course, it is possible to wrestle three points out of any text; however, in doing so, the text may be wrestled out of its context. Exposition must be true to context. Some expository sermons may follow what I call the "free-flow" form. That is, it freely moves through the text showing both what the text meant in the original setting with application for the twentieth century setting.

The Method of Preparation. In my judgment a sermon is not expository unless it deals with both what the text *meant* to the first readers and what it *means* for our application. To get at what the text meant calls for an in-depth, objective exegesis. The preparer must ask the following questions: (1) What does this text mean in its *literary context*? What is it doing here? In order to answer that he

20

must study the entire book that text is in until he understands its holistic approach. (In order to get the holistic understanding of the book, ask: What theme keeps coming up over and over? How does the book move? How does it hang together? What are the transition words? How do the various sections relate to the over-all movement?) Without doing this, it would be easy to make a text say what the original writer did not intend it to say. It is not enough to understand a text only in its immediate context. The wider the context that the preparer understands, the more accurate his exegesis will be.

(2) What is the *historical context* of the text? To find the answer to this question, another question must be asked over and over again in one's study—What is going on in the lives of the first readers that caused the original author to say this in this way? It is a very crucial question, for only as we sense the situation for which the text is intended can we make a proper application to a similar situation today.

Understanding the situation of the audience also calls for some research in the world of the New Testament. Some tools for this study would include: J. Jeremias. *Jerusalem in the Time of Christ*; N. Levison. *The Jewish Background of Christianity*; G. F. Moore. *Judaism*; A. Edersheim. *The Life and Times of Jesus the Messiah*; A. Edersheim. *Sketches of Jewish Social Life*; Daniel-Pops. *Daily Life in the Times of Jesus*; Bo-Reiche, *The New Testament Era*; R. Bultman. *Primitive Christianity*; C. K. Barrett. *The New Testament Backgrounds*; and *The New Testament Abstracts*.

(3) Understanding what the text meant also calls for the understanding of the *meaning of words* used. The poorest way to do this is by gleaning the word meaning from its

root. Just because the root of a word had one meaning when the word was first used, this does not mean that word still carries that same meaning. A word can have one connotation in one context which it would not have in another. Therefore, we must ask about its usage in the text we are using, its usage in the whole book, and also its usage by that author in other books. But we must also note whether or not the context is similar in the holistic view of the New Testament or the whole Bible.

However, we cannot allow the exact rendering in one context to dictate its meaning in another. We must study *how* the word is used in various places. The best tool for English readers is *Young's Analytical Concordance*. When using this book, do the following: (a) note the Greek (or Hebrew) word from which the English word came, (b) then go to the back of the book and find that Greek (or Hebrew) word and note each way it is translated, (c) then look up all the verses where the word appears.

For the Greek and Hebrew students, the best tool is Moulton and Geden's *Concordance to the Greek New Testament,* and Hatch and Redpath's *Concordance to the Septuagint.* Mandelkern, *Veteris Testament Concordantial Hebraical Atique Chaldaical* is also helpful. Comparing versions is good also.

Some of the following word studies would be helpful, but these should not be consulted until the student has done his own inductive research and analysis: *The Theological Dictionary of the New Testament* (9 vols.); *The Theological Dictionary of the Old Testament* (some vols. still in preparation); Alan Richardson. *A Theological Word Book of the Bible*; Deissman. *Light From the Ancient*

East; A. T. Robertson. *Word Pictures of the New Testament*; William Barclay. *New Testament Words* (also his commentaries).

(4) From understanding the word meaning, we must move to the word's place in the *grammatical setting*. Note carefully the conjunctions, transition words, and the verb tenses to see how the text hangs together.

When the preparer does all the above, he is ready to decide what the text was intended to mean to the first readers. This study must precede any exposition. *The International Critical Commentary* specializes in this approach, but this is only the first step in sermon preparation. He must also ask about the theological context of the text in order to apply meaning to his audience. This means a consideration of other biblical teachings about the subject and their interrelationships will be needed for clarification.

Now let us consider how to find out what the text *means* for application. We must communicate the "meantness" of the text in such a way that it does for the twentieth-century person what it was intended to do for the first-century reader. This means we have to know our audience, its situation, and its language. An expository sermon transfers the language of the first century into the language of the twentieth century. It bridges the gap of the historical situation of the first century and the situation of the twentieth century by meaningful application.

If we do not make *explanations* in the language people understand, they will not see the sense of the text. If we do not make *application*, they will not see the relevance of it. The application may be drawn throughout the sermon or at the end, but it certainly should be the type of application that the people can identify with (see themselves in that situation). In short, an expository sermon calls for

23

discovering what the text says, understanding what it meant, and personally applying it.

The Mechanics of Preparation. I obtain waste paper on which I have written on only one side or obtain some paper from a print shop, cut the paper into 3 x 5 cards, and use them for note-taking during my research. At the top left, I put the general topic; on the top right, I put the specific aspect of that topic. The body of the card I use for information gleaned. On the bottom or back I put the research source.

Example:

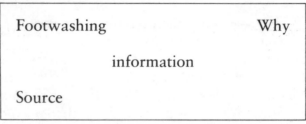

When writing on a particular text, I use the cards putting the text on the top left and the word I'm researching on the top right.

Example:

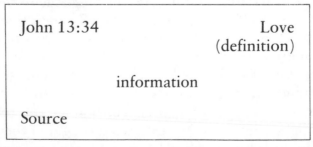

When I'm through with the research, I organize the cards by topic and text. My sermon is almost organized in this manner.

Then I decide on what form my sermon will take based upon its flow and my intention. I then proceed to write the exposition based upon the understanding of the text, its language, its historical situation, and upon my understanding of my audience.

Helps for Meaningful Study. To keep current in biblical studies, I would encourage the preacher to develop the following as a minimum in his daily schedule: Read ten pages of the New Testament, read five pages of the Old Testament, read one journal article, read one chapter in a pertinent book, spend two or three hours preparing (researching for) his sermon. If he can read Greek or Hebrew, also spend a half hour reading the Bible in that language.

Some journals that are helpful are: *Expository Times, Interpretation, Review and Expositor, Restoration Quarterly, New Testament Abstracts,* and *Old Testament Studies.*

Some helpful books are: Donker. *Multipurpose Tools For Bible Study*; Scholer. *A Basic Bibliographic Guide for New Testament Exegesis*; Kaiser and Kimmel. Exegetical Method; Job. *How to Study the Bible*; Vos. *Effective Bible Study.*

The preacher might be interested in knowing that the bookstore of Lincoln Christian College, Lincoln, Illinois, has a basic bibliography for preachers. The bookstore sells any book in that bibliography for 10% above cost. Many of the basic books for help in doing good exegesis are on that list. He should write for the list and begin to purchase wisely.

THE STRUCTURE OF THE EXPOSITORY SERMON

By W. F. Lown

Webster says, "A sermon is a discourse delivered in public, usually by a clergyman, for the purpose of religious instruction, and grounded on a passage of scripture." He goes on to say that it usually has to do with conduct or duty and "hence, an annoying harrangue," but there are two schools of thought on that evaluation!

Dr. Austin Phelps defined a sermon as, "An oral address to the popular mind, or religious truth contained in the scriptures, and elaborately treated with a view to persuasion."

Professor Conley Silsby has revised the Phelps definition to say, "A sermon is an oral message, studiously and prayerfully prepared for a particular congregation upon a religious theme as contained in the Christian scriptures, attractively presented with a view to indoctrination, inspiration or persuasion." If I were to revise this (and this thought may be implied by Professor Selsby) I would add "prepared *by a particular preacher* for a particular congregation. . . ." There is so much preaching today which is a mere regurgitation of what another preacher has written and foisted upon a given congregation in the sacred name of preaching.

Now we are to deal with the idea of the expository sermon—what it is and how it is structured. The expository sermon, one would conclude from reading the literature and from hearing preachers discuss the matter, is considered by many to be the most valuable and most drastically needed style of sermon structure. "Expository" means to expose, to shed light upon so a subject, an object, or a person is exposed to view. Expository preaching, then, should shed light on a subject or a biblical passage so that the Person Jesus Christ is clearly exposed to the listeners' view. There appears to be no more effective way to make Christ and His teachings known than by unfolding the meaning and exposing to view a portion of the Bible, the Word of God.

While there is much agreement as to the need for and the value of expository preaching, there is considerable diversity (perhaps the word in confusion!) as to what constitutes an expository sermon, or as to how to construct a gospel or biblical presentation in this form. H. Grady Davis says, "the terms topical, textual, and expository, are used loosely and not at all uniformly in homiletical literature, and are of limited usefulness" (p. 32).[1]

There is an ill-substantiated view that (1) topical sermons deal with a religious topic but utilize little or no scripture in the process, dealing largely with moral subjects; (2) that the textual sermon is a structure used to deal with presenting brief passages of scriptures; and (3) that the expository sermon is a structure used in the presentation of a long or extended passage.

The writer does not believe this rather loose delineation to be professional, adequate or even very helpful. May we offer instead the following proposed description of each structural classification: (1) the topical structure should indeed deal with a topic. However, it should be carefully consistent with Biblical teaching, and should make whatever use of Biblical references as will present the topic consistent with Scriptural teaching; (2) the textual structure may not explain a particular text at all, but may use the natural divisions of a given text to explain a particular

---

1. Grady H. Davis, *Design for Preaching*, Philadelphia: Fortress Press, 1958, p. 32.

topic; finally (3) the expository structure is the vehicle used to bring to the hearer's view the meaning of a given passage of scripture, whatever its brevity or length.

Let it be emphasized again that these structures are merely that—structures, and that in each case the deep and abiding truths of the Word of God must be presented by whatever style the preacher may select.

James S. Stewart has said,

> It cannot be too emphatically stated that if contemporary evangelism is to make its full impact on the secularism of this age, it will have to go back more constantly and deliberately than it has done, and also more patiently and humbly, to its own fountain-head in the New Testament, and test there its message to this generation, re-examining in that light the content, the claim, and the communication of its message.[2]

In another place Stewart rightly says, ". . . the greatest drag on Christianity today, . . . is not the secularism without, it is the reduced Christianity within. . . ."[3] This is what Kierkegaard called a "vaporized Christianity."

We are attempting to insist in this essay that, while we are speaking of *sermonic structure,* this must always be subservient to the fundamental call of our Lord to "preach the word." Whatever structure-type will best assist this in any given situation should be selected.

John A. Broadus, whose *Preparation and Delivery of Sermons*[4] is still a classic work in Homiletics after some

---

2. James S. Stewart, *A Faith to Proclaim*, New York: Scribner and Sons, 1953, p. 29.

3. *Op cit.*, p. 31.

4. John A. Broadus, *Preparation and Delivery of Sermons,* New York: Harper & Bros., 1870.

one hundred years, gives as the primary sermon classification system: doctrinal, moral, historical and experimental, but does in another place (Chapter V) classify "homiletical structures" as topical, textual and expository. He correctly and persistently insists, however, that structure must always be the secondary consideration. We have for years tried to impress upon students that the study of Homiletics is to introduce the student to "tools" rather than "rules."

Broadus says something which gives us the cue for our discussion of structure classification in this paper: "the distinction between subject-sermons and text-sermons has to do simply with the plan of the discourse, *especially with the source of its divisions*" (italics mine, W. F. L.). He proceeds. "Subject sermons are those in which the divisions are derived from the subject, independently of the text, while in text-sermons the divisions are taken from the text."[5]

With regard to the expository sermon Broadus says little more than that its name "is derived from . . . and that (it) is mainly occupied with exposition."[6]

Every homiletician must sooner or later struggle with the development of his own concepts of sermon structure. Hopefully those concepts should have as much uniformity as possible from one "technician" to another, yet each man's understanding must be meaningful in his own sermon workshop.

Let us now venture to construct a model by which to guide our attempted descriptions.

---

5. *Op cit.*, p. 133.
6. *Op cit.*, p. 141.

Sermon Structure Model

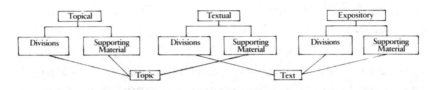

The reader will identify the three traditional sermon structure forms across the top of the model. Under each is plotted first, the divisions, then the materials assembled in support of those divisions. At the bottom of the model is the designation of the divisions and supporting material as to whether these are related to topic or text in the three traditional classifications.

The Topical Sermon

However the preacher defines and develops the topical sermon, all are essentially agreed that this type of structure deals with a given topic or subject. It is hoped that every sermon, whatever its structural style, will be consistent with biblical teaching and will employ biblical material to the maximum.

But how is the topical sermon put together structurally? First of all it will deal with a topic that is dealt with in the Bible. It may be selected because of its appearing in the scriptures or it may be selected because it is a practical problem in the life of a Christian or in the life of the church.

Secondly. its divisions (i.e., the "main points" of the sermon) will relate to the topic. Moreover, the supporting material (i.e., the subdivisions, the sub-subpoints, the illustrations, etc.) will be selected with a view to teaching the subject (topic) under consideration.

It will be noted that we are using the following terminology: "the divisions (or supporting material) are *related to* . . ." rather than *"selected from.* . . ."

Expository Sermons

Now to view the model (Fig. 1) again. Note in the right-hand section that in the expository sermon type structure the divisions will be related to (possibly, but not necessarily taken from) the text, and the supporting material will be chosen with a view to unveiling (exposing) the text under consideration.

In a word, the topical sermon is a structure designed to *teach a topic.* The expository sermon is a structure designed with a view to teaching the text—whatever its length.

Now in speaking of "teaching the text" we are not speaking of a verse-by-verse study of a passage. Those who try this are almost destined to failure and, thinking they have done expository preaching, give it up as a lost cause. One may "expose" the teaching of the text on a verse-by-verse basis, but this is not to be construed as an expository sermon structure. The expository sermon structure takes the passage to be considered, scrutinizes it for its main thought divisions (whatever the number) then uses *whatever material is available* from whatever source (the text, other references, history, literature, etc., etc.) to *teach the text*!

Textual Sermons

There is a lot of vagueness about all of the three structure-types, perhaps more especially the textual sermon. As we said earlier in this essay, there is a rather loose notion that textual sermons are to deal with short scripture passages

31

and expository sermons with long passages. We choose to reject this system of designation and devise the description represented in the model (Fig. 1).

In the very center of the model it will be noted that the divisions of the textual sermon are related to a text (probably actually taken from it, whether in exact or restated form). However, the purpose of the textual sermon is *to teach a subject,* and to use divisions found in a given text to do so. So, (see Fig. 1) the textual sermon has divisions which relate to a text, and supporting material selected with a view to teaching a topic or subject.

So the textual sermon is the homiletical "halfway house" between the topical and the expository structure, selecting characteristics from each.

While the following is something of an aside from our central consideration, it should be noted that some may take exception to our using the terms "topical" and "subject" interchangeably. We are doing this in this article, although we tend to use the term "subject" to describe what the sermon is *about,* and the term "topic" to refer to what the sermon is *called,* its name, in other words.

This article is supposed to present the expository sermon structure. We have only presented other structure forms to help differentiate the expository structure. It must be said again as a reminder: this presentation is the development of this writer and is not to be construed as a universally accepted concept, as C. S. Lewis said in concluding one of his books—this helps me. If it doesn't help you, forget it.

PREPARING AN EXPOSITORY SERMON

By E. Ray Jones

The procedure that I follow in preparing an expository sermon is not unique with me. It is a composite of all that I have studied through the years.

The first and essential step for effective preaching is that of the selection and thorough study of the Scripture to be used. The Scripture may be a chapter or only a paragraph. In the following message I used a rather lengthy passage. However as a rule I use only a few verses. Whatever selection is made one must do his best to understand the context, the significant words and the relationship of this passage to other teaching.

As one pours over the Scripture there begin to emerge certain points of emphasis. The great value of expository preaching for the local church and the weakness of it for publication is that each man will view the Scripture passage and see the application of the Word of God in his peculiar situation. Differing congregations will have different problems. So the application must relate to the need.

Following the study of the Scripture and the pulling out of the points, there must be a sound exegesis of the specific verses that are used. Sometimes this exegesis will be lengthy and at other times it will be short. However, before any forceful application can be made the particular point made must be scripturally grounded.

The next step is that of the application. Expository preaching is far more than a running verse by verse commentary. It is more than sound exposition. It is application in such a way as to relate Scripture to life.

One of the key points in effective application is the wise use of illustrations. It is for this reason that it is essential for the preacher not only to read widely but to be very observant. One does not read just for illustrations, but if reading is done out of a thirst for knowledge, illustrations will inevitably present themselves.

Expository preaching as all other forms of proclamation moves toward a conclusion that demands from the listeners a decision. Thus it is vital that the preacher, as he begins to speak, ask himself what decision he wishes those who hear him to make. If he is clear in his mind the message will move toward that end.

The purpose of this message is to point out that the apostle Paul gave visible evidence to the quality of his faith, by the way he reacted when that faith came under pressure. The reader must decide how well the message has succeeded in proving that point.

THE VALUE OF PREPARING EXPOSITORY SERMONS

By Sam E. Stone

Expository preaching is not easy—but it *is* worth the effort!

Expository preaching is biblical. It is sure to be true to the message when properly followed. Not only does it deal with the themes of scripture, but it grants them consideration proportionate to the space allotted them by divine intention.

It is satisfying. It cannot help but encourage a minister to bring God's message and watch it help people.

It is enriching. Think of the feeling of accomplishment. You preach through an entire New Testament book. You will always feel more at home here. It will build churches. People want and need Bible exposition.

But some preachers don't see it that way.

"Sure! In Bible college the professors tell you that expository preaching is best. But in the churches, people just won't take to it."

I heard that remark once too often. I decided to find out for myself and I think I did.

About ten years ago when I was preaching at the Western Hills Church of Christ in Cincinnati, I tested this procedure by making every sermon that I preached during a two month period an expository message. Sermons were based on I Timothy going consecutively through the book. Although I did not deal with every verse of the six chapters in the body of the sermons, I included the entire book in the selection of scriptures to be read aloud before the messages.

On the final day of the series, I took a casual, unofficial poll of the congregation to see if they would "take to it."

35

Each member was asked to give his candid opinion, writing it on the back of his roll call card. I honestly did not know what to expect. I asked three questions.

The first was, "Do you like this type of expository sermon series—going completely through a Bible book?" Of those who answered, eighty-two said "yes," three said, "no." One of these explained that, since she worked in children's church every other Sunday morning, she would prefer that the series of sermons be confined to the evening, so she could hear all of them!

Next, members were asked, "Why?" Their answers were solid and certain. The most frequent reason given was, "It helps me understand the Bible." (A fuller list of the replies follows later.)

Then, members were asked to indicate what book they would like to have treated in a future sermon series. The votes were: Romans, 15; James, 10; Hebrews, 8; and Ephesians and Revelation, 5 each.

What did this survey reveal? It assured me that, by this congregation at least, expository preaching is regarded not only as good, but as preferable to other styles. It indicated the people want to know what the Bible says.

This was not the first series of expository sermons used during the preceding four years of preaching at the Western Hills church. Earlier series had dealt with sections of Scripture such as the Beatitudes, the Ten Commandments, and the letters to the seven churches. Included were expository sermons on Philemon, 3 John, and Jude. Over a period of several Sunday nights, I allotted one sermon to each book.

Expository series on entire books or parts of books also had been used at either morning or evening services but never before at both.

Perhaps the most intensive undertaking up to this point was a series on the book of Acts, which ran for two quarters on Sunday nights. At that time members were asked not only to read the selected chapter before the service, but also to memorize a key verse from that section. The people indicated their appreciation of such a plan.

The series of messages from I Timothy differed from these in one important particular: it afforded one book exclusive continuous treatment at both morning and evening services.

The series demonstrated a number of important principles —some quite contrary to popular opinion.

(1) Expository preaching does not cause a decline in attendance. In fact, the attendance for morning worship services during this series averaged 408 as compared with 320 at this time the preceding year. Evening worship attendance likewise grew from an average of 161 the previous year to 209 that year.

(2) Expository preaching brings response to the gospel invitation. God blessed the congregation with twenty-two who came in answer to the invitation during the two-month period.

(3) People appreciate biblical messages for many reasons. Asked why they like expository series preaching, members replied:

"It encourages knowing the Word."

"For overall insight."

"It makes application along with an explanation of the verses. Very helpful to those not knowing much!"

"I feel it keeps one preaching on the Word."

"You keep one train of study and get more out of it than with just one sermon."

"Sunday School goes into this, but this way it seems to be more dynamic and lasting."

"Helps in retaining information. Keeps each week tied to the others."

"Fine—if each is complete and not dependent on the others."

"We like to make notes and refer to them in our Bible study at home."

"I think you have been able to touch on some things that might not have fit into a specific sermon otherwise."

"It gives the congregation a chance to study and become part of the message that is presented there."

Ben Merold told about an early misconception he had. He said, "I thought that an evangelist couldn't read and a Bible scholar couldn't preach! Later," he added, "I found that there was another alternative. You could *combine* zeal with knowledge!" He's right. The ideal preacher is one who can think with the philosopher and theologian, but speak in a language of the common man. Look at the men who have reached the most for Christ, built the largest churches, written the most popular books and composed the hymns and gospel songs that last the years. They are not trying to impress people with how many big words they know—but simply communicate Christ's truth. Someone remarked that many who seek to be profound succeed only in becoming polysyllabic!

We've all known professors who could take something simple and make it hard to figure out. But the really great teacher, in my estimation, is the one who can take a difficult topic and make it understandable. This should be our goal as preachers—to help men understand God's word.

Expository preaching helps the minister to do this. He may plan ahead in his work. He may buy books and take special courses to equip him for dealing with a given biblical book. He comes to know that portion of scripture more fully and interpret it more accurately. He can preach on vital themes which might otherwise be overlooked or omitted. He brings the "whole counsel of God."

An older minister told me as I began to preach, "I don't know what I would do if I had to think of a topic every Sunday. I know I would run dry in a hurry. I don't see how a preacher can stay fresh and creative unless he practices expository preaching."

It is true, of course, that no two ministers are alike. No one method may be suitable for every minister in every church on every Sunday. I would ask this, however: Let a minister try expository preaching before he rejects it. Let churches ask their minister for this type of solid, planned presentation and grant it a fair hearing.

Such messages need not lack for variety. Sermons may be biographical, textual, topical, etc., and still be expository. An expository sermon is recognized by the fact that it is based on a passage of scripture—whether one verse or many. It attempts to explain the correct meaning of the passage and to apply it forcefully and convincingly to the audience. It must relate to men.

It may serve one of many purposes. The sermon on Romans 1:16 and 17 used as an example in this book is an introductory message for a series of sermons studying through the book of Romans. It is designed to introduce and give a background for the book.

Expository sermons need not be lengthy. A capable pulpiteer need not weight his outline with footnotes on every commentary reference. Certainly he need not go verse by verse through an entire chapter in one message. Who says expository preaching must be dull? True exposition breathes the very life of God into a gasping, dying world. It revives! It renews life! It meets the practical, pertinent, pressing needs of men.

Expository preaching *is* hard. It *is* rough. But it is worth the effort! What will it cost you to preach expository sermons? Here is a brief survey:

(1) It costs disciplined study to determine the author's meaning in a passage as revealed by the original language. If you are skilled in Greek, this may be easy for you. For most of us, it requires work.

(2) It costs dollars in buying commentaries and studies for the book at hand. Popular sermon books may seem to be less expensive.

(3) It takes time to break down a six-chapter epistle into units of thought—each suitable for a message.

(4) It is not easy to discuss some of the topics which come up—e.g. woman's place, or paying the minister (from I Timothy).

(5) It may challenge your unequivocal loyalty to the status quo of the Restoration movement. For example: Is the minister of today pictured in I Timothy? Does your church have a roll of widows (I Timothy 5:9)?

(6) It costs you sleep when you know that you must produce a sermon on the already-announced passage of Scripture for the next Sunday! That sermon barrel never looks so good as it does when it is off limits!

(7) It demands an agonizing search to find penetrating, pertinent, practical illustrations to enrich and enliven your presentation. You need humor, poetry,

40

modern-life stories, biblical background, anecdotes—
all of the factors which go into any good sermon.
And you must find the ones that fit this passage.

Preparing expository sermons is the finest way to preach.
That majestic pulpit master, F. B. Meyer, declared: "Expository preaching is the consecutive treatment of some book
or extended portion of scripture on which the preacher
has concentrated head and heart, brain and brawn, over
which he has thought and wept and prayed, until it has
yielded up its inner secret, and the spirit of it has passed
into this spirit."

ESSAY ON SERMON PREPARATION

By Douglas A. Dickey

Asking a preacher how he prepares sermons is a little like asking an artist how he paints pictures or a poet how he writes poems. Not that all preachers are artistic and poetic, but there is always something in any man's method of preparation and preaching that wholly eludes description.

A recent issue of the Readers Digest[1] tells of a time when Robert Frost was sitting for a portrait by sculptor Joe Brown. One of Browns' students asked Frost, "How do you go about writing a poem?"

Frost answered, "Well, first, something has to happen to you. Then you put some words on a piece of paper and ride them like a horse until you have a poem." This was Frost's attempt to answer the elusive question, and my answer can be structured roughly among the same lines.

The classic formula for expository preaching urges the preacher to begin with the text. It must be analyzed, understood, listened to and exegeted before one can preach its message. That time-honored approach would seem to conflict with Frost, who says "something must happen to you." I'm not so sure a conflict exists here, at least not in my experience. It is true that an expository sermon is by definition not expository unless it "exposes" a text, but the question is really, how does one come to an understanding of the text in the first place?

In his important little book, *The Integrity of Preaching*[2] John Knox says that truly biblical preaching must be both biblical and relevant. We are accustomed to create a rather sharp dichotomy here. In general, we have believed

---

1. *Reader's Digest,* July 1974, p. 36.
2. John Knox, *The Integrity of Preaching,* Abingdon Press.

and taught in our particular movement that being biblical is far more important than relevancy, which can lead one into subjectivism and the often despised "topical preaching."

Knox helped me greatly at this point. He says biblical preaching is not biblical simply because it is larded with biblical references, or even because it has clear insights into the original meaning of the text. Such preaching can be most unbiblical in the sense that it is not directed, as the biblical message *always* is, to some particular and contemporary situation. On the other hand preaching which is meant to be relevant is not so simply because it reveals a knowledge of contemporary events and makes sophisticated reference to them. Knox quotes a magazine article in which a woman relates her reason for turning from the church. She said she did so because the church seemed to her to have lost contact with both the first century *and* the twentieth century.[3] Knox goes on to say that, in his view, truly biblical preaching will always be relevant, and truly relevant preaching will always be biblical.

Also instructive to me at this point have been the writings and sermons of Harry Emerson Fosdick. His very name was enough, during the early days of my preaching in the thirties, to arouse cries of "modernism." However, in my opinion, Fosdick represents a real watershed in the history of preaching. He tells in his autobiography,[4] about the style of preaching in his early days being almost exclusively based on the objective exposition of the scriptural text with scarcely any reference to the needs of people. Fosdick said he finally decided that people did not come to church

---

3. *Ibid.*, p. 24.
4. Harry Emerson Fosdick, *The Living of These Days.*

"desperately anxious to hear what happened to the Jebu-
sites."[5]

He began to structure his sermons around the needs of
people which had become known to him through his coun-
seling and pastoral experience. He began with the problem,
and led into the text, and in so doing started a whole new
philosophy of preaching.

Admittedly there is the danger here of distorting or totally
ignoring the scriptural basis of genuine biblical preaching. However, if one reads Fosdick's sermons today (and
they are easily available in several volumes) one is impressed with the unique and powerful combination of
biblical content and contemporary application which they
represent.

I refer to all of this to give some background to my conviction that Frost is right in saying that in creating a poem,
or a sermon, first "something must happen to you."

What happens may be an encounter with the text. Some
old and well-worn text may leap with life because of some
experience of the expositor which opens him up to new
meanings which had previously eluded him. What happens
may be an experience or an event or an encounter which
brings a man back to a text to give meaning to the experience. How does one begin to prepare an expository sermon?
If it is to be more than a dry and academic lecture on
biblical background, something must happen to a man.
Sometimes it happens while he is faithfully studying the
text, sometimes when he is driving the car or mowing the
lawn or reading the newspaper. I am not saying that one
must always have some uplifting subjective experience in

---

5. *Ibid.*, p. 92.

order to preach. Sometimes one must preach when nothing seems to have happened, when the well is dry and, as Frederick Kershner used to say, "The chariot wheels drag slowly through the mud." Perhaps in such times the negative experience and the emotional dryness itself may lead one to a text and a meaning which will be of particular help to people who must themselves spend many days of their lives living without inspiration and dealing with the "quiet desperation" of which Thoreau speaks.

In any case, it is my contention that a sermon, to be truly expository, must be based both in the text and in some experience which is related to it.

Then, how does one "ride it like a horse" until a sermon is produced? Many men have many methods. Some are writing-oriented and they must get the words in manuscript form. Others are speaking-oriented, and they must shape the words for extemporaneous delivery. My own method is the latter, and my routine is somewhat as follows.

Once the text, or the idea, has taken some life in my mind, I begin to write down ideas, quotations, possible illustrations, alternative translations of the text, ideas from the Greek—anything and everything that occurs to me, and, (this is important) *without any reference to order or outline,* at least at first.

Such an "incubating" process may take hours, days or weeks. At some point, after "sleeping on it," allowing the subconscious to operate (and I think prayer is often allowing God to speak through the subconscious)—an outline takes shape. In my preparation, the outline is all-important. It must, to be alive, shape itself out of the material, and not be imposed upon the material. I have done it both ways, but when I abort the birth of the sermon

45

by imposing an outline upon it too soon, I kill its spontaniety.

Then, I memorize the outline, and go over it in my mind again and again, "riding the horse" until it takes on a kind of organic wholeness and a natural flow of ideas.

Delivery of the sermon then, for me, is without notes, or with a few scraps of paper to keep quotations and references accurate. This is what I mean by "extemporaneous" —not without preparation, but without written manuscript or extensive notes at the time of delivery.

For years I felt guilty about this method, especially when I talked to the "manuscript type" preacher who writes out every word before delivery. I no longer feel guilty, having decided that the method fits my peculiar mind and personality.

Sometimes, in the delivery, the whole thing, or large parts, are changed. Whole sections I planned to preach are left out, or new ideas and illustrations come during delivery. In recent years I have become very conscious of the need for *timing*, believing now that most sermons are too long. Expository preaching can concentrate so minutely upon the text, and upon the preacher's own self-centered interpretation of it, that almost nothing is communicated to the hearer. It is usually such a situation that results in an over-long sermon, or at least one that seems too long. If one does his best to think and feel his way into the text, and to do the same into the situation and problems of his hearers, then the sermon can truly communicate, which, after all, is the aim and purpose of all preaching. In other words, sensitive empathy with the hearer is just as important as faithful exposition of the text.

John R. W. Stott expresses this same conviction in a recent interview:

I've often said that I think there is a most tragic polarization in the church today. Evangelicals on the whole, are happy on one side of the divide. They love the Bible; they live in the Bible; they study the Bible. But most of their preaching is up in the air. It's exposition without application. It isn't earthly because many evangelicals are uncomfortable in the modern world. They have rejected the modern world.

And to complete the polarization: a liberal ecumenical person is happy on the other side of the divide. He is a modern man. But he's lost the Bible. And I think we need to pray and work towards the rise of a new generation of communicators who are equally proficient in both.[6]

I heartily agree with Stott's analysis, and the above is my attempt to suggest in general how I go about trying to approach this ideal.

---

6. John R. W. Stott, Interview in *Mission*, "Crisis In Preaching," Abilene, Texas, May 1974, p. 9.

SERMON PREPARATION

By Orval M. Morgan

The homoletical pattern followed by any one person will reflect two things—his knowledge of the general laws of homiletics, and his own personal adaptation of these laws to his own use. It is well established that a man is not to become a slave to rules per se, but must be the master of them and thus be guided and helped by them. For my use and assistance, I have formed certain homiletical procedures which I follow without much variation.

At the outset let me say that I strongly favor an over all preaching pattern. Sermon projection is the heart of this plan. For general purposes, I work on a long time basis, perhaps five years. In this plan the needs of the congregation must be known, and used in the projection. With this in mind, a yearly theme may be chosen, and then broken down into segments befitting your purpose and plan.

For example, we will suppose your people need stress on doctrinal matters and you set aside a year in which to attack this need. You can divide your emphasis into quarters or according to your plan of presentation. Let's take a concrete example. List seven rather large and general areas you want to stress: God, Christ, the Holy Spirit, the Word of God, Stewardship, Evangelism, and Faithfulness. Having done this you will need to outline 12 messages dealing with each of these areas, for you will preach on each of these fields once each month for twelve months, assuming you have morning and evening services. You will have ample opportunity to plot your point of teaching in each case and give wide variety to the type of sermons you preach. As you note, one Sunday each month is left open to take care of any special matters that need attention.

Having drawn up your general pattern, it is then necessary to work out the specifics. I have done this by a system of study which allowed me to spend 15 hours on the sermons for each Lord's Day. This requires a rigid discipline and begins by being in the study at 7:00 a.m. and continuing uninterruptedly until 10:30 a.m. five days a week. Emergency calls and death being the only valid reasons for interruption. This permitted me to work on ten messages each week—beginning on Monday in the preparation of the two messages I was to preach five weeks hence. Tuesday morning I took up the messages I had started the previous Monday and developed them still further. On Wednesday, the sermons started on Monday three weeks back were the object of my study. Then on Thursday and Friday I spent the time on the messages I was to preach on the coming Lord's Day. This plan gave me ample time to read, research, and brood on and over the sermons. Illustrations would come to mind during this period and the subconscious mind beame your benefactor. Many rebel at a plan such as this and give what they feel to be legitimate excuses for not using it. To me it all depends on your view of your task as a minister of the Gospel. By following this program I found I could put my main aim, preaching, first and still find time for all the other duties of the ministry.

Having established your protection and pattern, you turn to the business of sermon preparation. We are to preach the Word with an effort to win the lost and edify the saints. This involves two rather different approaches. The former must present Christ, his life, death, burial and resurrection as the Gospel power able to save man. The latter must deal with the ethics of the Christian system and will present more the teaching of Christ and the Epistles.

I have found many men who hammer on "first principles" to a congregation in which few if any are alien sinners. While it is necessary to preach the plan God has for man, we must evaluate the opportunity before us and use it to God's best interest.

Some men seem to have a hard time finding sermon materials and resort to preaching canned sermons. This type of preaching seldom gets the job done. Usually, whatever denominational man's sermons are preached, they end up making that kind of denominational people. Why do this when the Word is our garden and richly supplied with material of great sermonic value? Many men follow topical preaching almost exclusively and justify it by the worn out excuse of lack of time to do any thing else. Topical preaching has its place, a small place in my thinking. It consists most of what the preacher thinks or feels about a given topic, and the child of God needs to know what God has said about the matter.

Textual sermons are a step up the ladder and serve a real purpose in preaching. At least the main points come from the text and based on the proposition from that text a fence is set up that will keep the preacher in bounds, to say the least.

Expository preaching builds great churches and makes great preachers. Some shy away saying it is too much work and takes too much time. This means, generally, they do not know how it is done or that laziness has set in. In the expository sermon all the main and subpoints come from the text, supported by related scripture. To help in this type of sermon preparation, a factual data sheet is imperative. For a chapter on this I would call your attention to Chapter 9 in "Expository Preaching Without Notes" by C. W. Koller.

Let us turn now to the actual sermon preparation. I have been asked to present my method. Here you find I have adapted my plan and made it part of me, yet following the laws of Homiletics. This is what I feel each man has to do. I use a pattern of twelve steps.

1. Select Subject - and, or - Theme, Text
2. Analyze the text

Brood over it, my expression is "soak the beans." This comes from the practice of my mother who always put the beans to soak the night before she cooked them.

3. Form a solid proposition
4. Form your objective
5. Establish main points from text
6. Work out supporting points - sub-points
7. Select illustrations in keeping with message
8. Prepare conclusion
9. Prepare the introduction
10. Make a general, comprehensive outline
11. Prepare pulpit outline
12. *PREACH* the sermon

We will now consider each of these steps in some detail. As we keep in mind our overall plan and read the Word devotionally from day to day, subjects and texts come rather easily. In the text used for the sermon printed herewith, I found a large area for emphasis. It can be approached as a message on God's grace, the Gospel plan, incentives for Christian growth and faithfulness, and the evangelistic thrust of the grace of God. So we select Titus 2:11ff.

When I analyze a text, I take it apart, following the rule of Hermeneutics and Exegesis, being very sure to let God say what He intends to say. This is of primary importance. Several translations are read, as well as the original language. All my thoughts are written down as I go along and always kept for future use. A work sheet is a valuable piece of sermonic property. The steps usually given for the development of a text are employed, namely, explanation, argumentation, application and illustration. I carry a small note pad on which I write thoughts that may occur to me during the day on the text I am studying. As indicated above, you put the beans to soak and reap a rich harvest of ideas. I do not make it a practice to consult any commentator until I have exhausted the text from my own study. Then I may read what some scholar has written about the passage, remembering I am responsible for what I teach, not what he has said.

Some texts fall apart much easier than others, but I do not believe we should shun any text because it appears difficult. One thing must control our selection and study of a text. It must contain one complete thought. There may be others, but we are interested in that one complete idea.

During this study, sometimes early and sometimes late, will come your proposition. A proposition is a simple, clear, concise, declarative statement of what you propose to do *in* this sermon. It is your message in a nut shell and is absolutely necessary in every sermon. If you do not know where you are going, how can those who listen know? It will be a fence to keep you in bounds. It will find its proof in your text. When I find a sermon weak I always look to my proposition first. And I generally find my trouble.

Closely related to the proposition is the objective of the sermon. In stating it you must word it in a simple, clear, concise, declarative statement, and it will indicate what you propose to do *with* the sermon. This determination is governed by the proposition, the particular thrust you have in mind, and the way you develop your idea. It can include one of many areas of emphasis. It may show an evangelistic thrust, a devotional, a doctrinal, or exhortation, but whatever, it is the chief aim of the sermon, the bull's eye toward which you are aiming.

Having spent all this time, you will no doubt be able to select your main points with ease. They must be true to the text and support your proposition. How many do I want? Enough to fully develop my theme and no more. All the way from one point to seldom, if ever, more than four. I have found it best to make a complete sentence when wording a main point in my study. Things must be clear and if you are not clear enough to write out your main point, it may not be clear to you or any one else.

Almost at the same time you are working on the main points, sub-points will fall into place. But they need development and study. Here again do not use more than are needed to support the main point. I write these out also to help keep things simple and clear.

As this process has been going on, illustrations usually have come to me. These come from life experiences, reading and best of all from the Word. I keep a file of illustration and they are readily available as I select the pictures with which I want to make the message clear. Some are greatly tempted to plagiarize at this point. I feel you can use illustrations you have heard, but always tell them like you heard them and not as though they happened to you. Your audience generally is far ahead of you at this point.

It is my observation that the most neglected and poorly prepared part of the sermon is the conclusion. This must not be. This is why I have found it best, while the main and sub-points are still fresh in my mind, to prepare the conclusion. This is the pay off of the message, the call for action, the challenge to move. There are certain factors that are present in the conclusion. We have spoken of the objective of the sermon, this more or less determines the thrust of the conclusion. You know what you are "shooting" at and have through the presentation of your sermon brought your listeners to that point where they are being called upon to make some kind of a decision. Many times we forget the strength of motive appeal. By this I mean the drive within the person which you are going to use. It may be reward, loyalty, confirmation, fear or more than two hundred others. But you will want to use one. Sometimes it takes me a while to determine just what motive appeal to use. So much depends on the audience, the setting, and what I am driving towards. Having selected one, I recap my main points either literally or in generalities and choose the one which fits my purpose and motive appeal. Then with the use of persuasion and emotions, I challenge my audience.

It has been my conviction for many years that we have lost the art of exhortation. Many have never witnessed it being used. I have and what a power it is! In the light of this I have studied literature put out on exhortation and persuasion and tried to incorporate it into my method. It has been most rewarding.

Having rounded out my argument and formed my conclusion, I am now ready to consider how best to introduce my message to the congregation and how best to introduce them to the message. There are many ways of doing this, and to use the same method all the time is not only monotonous, but fatal to a good sermon. I learned long ago that no introduction should hold forth more than you are able to deliver. I have considered the old homiletic teaching of A. I. D. to be valid in an introduction, this means— secure *attention*; arose *interest*; and create *desire* to listen. One item that I have found very helpful is to memorize the first sentence of my introduction. This gets me off to a good start.

I am now ready to put the whole thing together in a logical order. In doing this I make a detailed outline of the whole sermon. From this, if necessary, I can write my sermon in manuscript form. It also is there for any future use, complete in each detail. I have found this valuable and I file it away with my folder that contains my work sheets, random ideas, etc. It will be there for ready reference.

For my pulpit outline, I use a very brief outline containing a notation of text, proposition and objective. I include the first sentence of the introduction and perhaps a word or two that will remind me of further thoughts to be used there. I use Romans for my main points and Arabic for subpoints. If others are needed, I use the alphabet. These points are much abbreviated, just enough there to guide me in my train of thought. Illustrations are noted by their main point or a line that reminds me what it is all about. The first and last sentences of the conclusion are always written out so I will be sure to launch into it with certain knowledge.

This further word about pulpit outline. If you have put the time in on the sermon as I have indicated, you pretty well know the outline from memory and will not be tied or bound to it. I have had a few times in my ministry when the lights went out and I had to go right ahead with the sermon. It is best to be prepared! If you have been able to get the sermon into your heart, then you can get into the sermon and with a great feeling of satisfaction and ease deliver a message in fine style and a convincing manner.

A closing word is offered in the light of experience, both past and present. I am alarmed by the apologetic way so many sermons are delivered these days. I believe every sermon should be PREACHED. If you have prepared something to say, and it is worth saying, then stand up and say it in love to the glory of God. Perhaps the greatest enemy to good preaching is the lack of discipline on the part of the preacher who finds time for everything except sermonic preparation. As His spokesman, we must not fail Him, our audience nor ourselves.

HOW I PREPARE TO PREACH

By Don H. Sharp

The preparation of a sermon is an awesome task. The necessity of having something to say each week, week after week, is oftentimes seen by the preacher as the Sword of Damocles hanging by a single hair over his head ready, at any moment, to do him in. Fortunately, most preachers do not view preaching or its preparation as a threat, but rather, as an opportunity to make a difference for the better in the lives of those who have ears to hear. Believing that the preaching of God's Word is a means which God uses to lift people from old ways of shame and despair to new ways of forgiveness and victorious living—the preacher plunges into his task with the same joy as a boy jumping into his favorite summer swimming hole.

Preaching, to be preaching, must be designed to instruct, comfort, correct, challenge, or inspire. My first step, therefore, in preparing to preach is to determine what will be the controlling purpose of my message. What, with God's help, should I hope to accomplish in preaching to those that will assemble? A sermon without a controlling purpose is like the big locomotive sitting in Washington's Smithsonian Institution Museum. It is an authentic steam engine with a recording in it that gives it the sound of steam, whistle and motion but that big engine never moves anywhere. It impresses the onlookers who stop for a minute, look and listen, then they go on their own way to other sights. Seeing that big locomotive in that setting was sort of sad, because you know at one time its sound was its own; it breathed with power and moved toward exciting destinations. Sermons should have power and move toward exciting destinations, or they become like museum engines, fit for nothing more than as reminders of past life and power.

Having established a controlling purpose, my next step in sermon preparation is the development of the theme. Let's say my purpose is to urge Christians to think and act more positively and less negatively: to move from pessimism to optimism. To develop this theme I put a call to worship together from related Scriptures which I have read and studied from a Nave's Topical Bible. Topics from the Nave's Topical Bible which would be related to a Christian's pessimism would be "Unbelief," "Doubt," and "Murmering." On the other hand, topics related to optimism would be such topics as "Faith," "Hope," and "Contentment." Such a study of the Word helps to pull the Scriptures together to give light on the desired theme. Having read what the Scriptures say I next look up related topics under material I have used and filed, along with material in such books as, "The New Dictionary of Thoughts," the Synopticon of the "Great Books of the Western World." This study helps me see what others have thought and said on the subject. Having put the raw materials in, I then trust the Holy Spirit to help me put together that which is relevant to my predetermined controlling purpose. Sometimes my study changes the purpose; I assume that by this change God has moved to re-direct my intent to be in keeping with His intent. Though the purpose may change radically enough cannot be said about the importance of that controlling purpose, it is a must.

Words are most important in preaching. Sermons must not be unclear, obscure or vague. For this reason I always have at hand a dictionary of synonyms so that my hearers may be spared, not only the boredom of repetitive words but that I might use words which transmit the message through the five senses—this of course is called sensory language. This writer feels strongly about using words which appeal to the senses. It is communication which involves the hearer's whole being.

The sermon must have a frame thus the necessity of an outline. As a house must be framed in before it is roofed, insulated, and closed in so must a sermon have an outline on which all the rest is added. The outline gives the sermon the strength to stand—to make sense.

Having outlined the message this writer proceeds to develop each point in full manuscript. Manuscript, at least for me, is a discipline to say what I want to say in the time slot allowed without being repetitive, ambiguous and astraying afar off into deadend side streets.

With an abiding conviction that preaching still is "the power of God unto salvation" I, for one, will continue to look forward to carefully preparing scripturally-centered messages which follow a definite theme and are designed to accomplish a purpose for so long as there is one person who will listen. The time may come when men will not have access to hear God's Word, but until that time let the men of God be faithful unto that which God has committed unto them, for it is required of a steward that he be found faithful.

PREPARING TO PREACH

By Charles R. Gresham

How do I prepare to preach? This is a question difficult to answer. Much preparation has already taken place in the very development and direction of one's life. There is also residual preparation in all the academic preparation of the past and the varying experiences growing out of the relationships sustained with people.

But, the question focuses more on that immediate preparation necessitated by a given sermon or address. How do I prepare week in and week out, for that responsible task of sharing sermonically with the people of God gathered for worship and service? This question is more specific, and, therefore, can be answered more specifically.

Allow me to suggest specific answers under three headings: (1) the Word of God in preparation; (2) the People of God in preparation; (3) The Man of God in preparation.

The Word of God in Preparation

The Word is the source of preaching. It not only gives the parameters relative to the task but it becomes the source of content for the task. Preparation, then, must begin in exposure to, immersion in, and imbibing of the Word. When the Word has become part of us ("Let the word of Christ dwell in you richly" —Col. 3:16a), we are able to reach back into this rich resource for illustrative material, adjunct ideas, etc., which will enhance our grasp of our theme and make our presentation more full-orbed.

But, the Word must be shared in some kind of orderly or systematic fashion. I have found that this is done best by preaching in series and by following an expository approach. Even great topics can be handled expositorily.

60

For example, "Worship" as a topic, can be approached with an expository treatment of Isaiah 6 and "Salvation" can be exposed through a similar treatment of Titus 3:4-8.

Once the series had been determined (and I believe there needs to be variety; moving from New Testament to Old Testament, from Book studies to topical or thematic series), then intensive study of the passages involved follows. Here the basic Bible Study tools come into the picture: dictionaries, word study volumes, even commentaries. Comparison with published sermons on these same passages is certainly in order, for certain ideas, illustrations, etc., can be gleaned from these sources, made one's own and used effectively in preaching.

I have found that illustrative material for biblical themes comes from many sources—collections of quotations, great classic literature, hymnody, religious poetry, current publications—both religious and non-religious (the *Readers Digest* can be a constant and fruitful source). Such illustrative material, used effectively, brings home the biblical truth vividly.

Structure is important. As one studies the passage that will be the source of the sermon, he needs to ask himself, What, in this passage, is being emphasized? How can I relate it structurally to my people? A sermon is not a running verse-by-verse, commentary of a biblical text. It is a structured discourse exposing and applying the truth of that text. The commentary lies behind the sermon and the sermon presupposes the exegesis; but the sermon is not mere exegesis.

Structure is the framework of the sermonic building. It should not be completely exposed, yet it should be there as in the outline of the building. As in any building, too

61

many sides, levels, gables, etc., become disconcerting; so in the sermon many points, sub-points, etc., may become distracting and confusing. Simplicity in structure is to be desired. There is still something to say for the old homiletical "three-point" approach, though, it certainly need not be rigidly followed.

The People of God in Preparation

If the Word is the source of our preaching, God's people are the context of that preaching. Gustaf Wingren notes significantly that "when the Bible lies open on the preacher's desk and the preparation of the sermon is about to begin, the worshipers have already come in; the passage contains these people since it is God's word to His people" (*The Living Word*, Philadelphia: The Fortress Press, 1960, p. 26).

It is at this point that relevance becomes significant. As we prepare, we must constantly ask, "How is this truth related to my hearers?" What does it say to our contemporary culture? These questions cannot be answered unless we know our people intimately and are aware of the cultural situation of which they are a part.

Preparation in this realm moves beyond the study. We can, in the study, learn of our culture; but we do not get the genuine feel and impact of it in such isolation. We must be "out" where our people are. This is also where the pastoral accompaniment of our preaching finds its focus. Sharing with our people in their ordinary lives as well as those crisis periods not only enhances our preaching but gives us insight to make our sermons more meaningful and "on target." As someone has said, "Preaching is never naked." It must be clothed with cultural understanding and pastoral relationship.

The Man of God in Preparation

The man who would preach spends a lifetime in preparation. His intellectual development, his spiritual growth, his awareness and sensitivity to persons and his understanding of the age are all part of that preparation. This is foundational.

But more specifically, the preacher prepares week by week for his task. In most instances, he will have two messages to prepare and, possibly, one or more teaching sessions (such as his Midweek Bible Study). To prepare for all these presentations, the preacher must use his time wisely.

I have found that Monday morning is the time to begin (I recognize that many preachers take Monday off, thus allowing the tension and pressure of the Lord's Day to dissipate). On the Lord's Day, you reach a mountain peak and the momentum is high. I find that Monday morning is my most productive time—not only as a result of this sense of momentum but also because by getting the sermon ready for the following Sunday early, some of the pressure toward the end of the week is relaxed.

Usually, I try to complete the Sunday morning sermon on Monday and try to have the evening sermon ready by Wednesday. Later in the week, I will go over these so that they will be fresh in my mind on the Lord's Day.

I have found a detailed outline is the most useful tool for me. By this means, the structure is clearly seen; and if there is a demand for publication of the sermon, you have a very useful beginning in this full outline. In my situation, the morning service is broadcast on the radio and the time period is quite constricted. A full outline allows one to operate within this time limitation in an excellent manner.

In addition to this weekly preparation for specific sermons, I am constantly building for future preparation as I clip poetry, illustrations, ideas, etc., and file them for future reference. Occcasionally, in this process, an idea will become so appealing (and will relate to a specific congregational need) that I may interrupt a current series of sermons by using a sermon prepared around this idea.

Above all, such preparation needs to be bathed in prayer. If a sermon has been prepared in prayer and is presented in prayer, then the promise of God will surely be fulfilled—"My word shall not return unto me void."

EXPOSITORY PREACHING FOR TODAY

By Don DeWelt

1. Identity
2. Form
3. Development
4. Illustration

How To Identify The Expository Sermon

Almost everyone agrees to the advantage of and need for expository preaching, but not all agree as to just what it is. Let's consider a few definitions and offer one of our own.

1. *Harold Knott*: "The expository sermon is an effort to explain, illustrate and apply the Scripture to life."

2. *F. B. Meyer*: "Expository preaching is the consecutive treatment of some book or extended portion of Scripture on which the preacher has concentrated head and heart, brain and brawn, over which he has thought and wept and prayed, until it has yielded up its inner secret, and the spirit of it has passed into his spirit."

3. *D. W. Cleverley Ford*: "What is expository preaching? It is uncovering hidden treasure. The word the disciples on the Emmaus Road used was *dianoiro*, meaning 'to open.' The scriptures are a closed book and it is the task of the minister of Christ to open the book. He is to open up the ground and expose the treasure."

4. *Faris D. Whitesell*: "An expository sermon is based on a Bible passage, usually longer than a verse or two; the theme, the thesis and major and minor divisions coming from the passage; the whole sermon being an

honest attempt to unfold the true grammatical-historical-contextual meaning of the passage, making it relevant to life today by proper organization, argument, illustrations, application and appeal."

5. *Andrew W. Blackwood*: "Expository preaching means that the light for any sermon comes mainly from a Bible passage longer than two or three consecutive verses."

6. *T. H. Pattison*: ". . . the topical sermon, in which the theme is especially prominent; the textual sermon, in which more regard is paid to the words of the text; and the expository sermon, in which, as a rule, a longer portion of the Bible is taken as the basis for the discourse."

7. *John A. Broadus*: "An expository discourse may be defined as one which is occupied mainly, or at any rate very largely, with the exposition of Scripture."

8. *Harry Jeffs*: "Exposition is the art of opening up Scriptures, laying them out, reproducing their matter and their spirit in forms vitalized by the personality of the expositor. . . . The main purpose of exposition is to apply the knowledge of Scripture to serviceable uses. The skill is perfected by practice."

9. *R. Ames Montgomery*: "The expository preacher purposes above everything else to make clear the teaching and content of the Bible. . . . The preacher seeks to bring the message of definite units of God's Word to his people. He discovers the main theme or constituent parts of a book's message as they were in the mind of the writer. These he unfolds step by step until he reaches the ultimate goal."

10. *Donald Grey Barnhouse*: "Expository preaching is the art of explaining the text of the Word of God, using all the experience of life and learning to illuminate the exposition."

Perhaps the best way to define is to illustrate. But before we offer an illustration of what we mean, we will state in as few words as possible what we mean by an expository sermon: *An expository sermon is that sermon in which the total outline is derived from the text. The theme, the main divisions, the subdivisions and all developments are a development of the text.*

We can best define by illustration and comparison. If we were to prepare a sermon from Romans 1:1-7, a *topical* outline might look like this:

Text: Rom. 1:1-7
Theme: The Bond Servant of Christ
Proposition: Characteristics of this Bond Servant

  I. He was urgent.
    A. In season
    B. Out of season
 II. He was profitable.
    A. To Man
    B. To God
III. He was rewarded.
    A. Here
    B. Hereafter

A *textual* outline would read like this:

Text: Rom. 1:1-7
Theme: Divine Greetings
Proposition: A consideration of the content of such a greeting

I. It concerned Paul, vs. 1a
   A. Called by God
   B. Used by God
   C. Rewarded by God

II. It concerned the Gospel, vs. 1b-3a
   A. It is good news.
   B. It is powerful.
   C. It needs to be preached.

III. It concerned His Son, vs. 3b-5a
   A. Son of man
   B. Son of God
   C. Son of righteousness

IV. It concerned those at Rome, vs. 5b-7
   A. Suffered persecution
   B. Spread the gospel
   C. Beloved of Paul

What distinction do you note in the two outlines? If you will look closely you will note that in the first example only the theme comes from the text; the proposition is formed from the theme only, *not the theme through the text*. There are many things we can say about Paul, and the topical sermon sets forth some of them.

In the textual sermon the proposition and main division are a development from the text; *the subdivisions are not*.

Here is an *expository* outline of this text:

Text: Rom. 1:1-7
Theme: Divine Greetings
Proposition: A consideration of the content of such a greeting

68

I. It concerns Paul, vs. 1a.
   A. A bond servant of Christ Jesus
   B. Called to be "one sent." (apostle)
   C. Separated unto the gospel

II. It concerns the Gospel, vs. 1b-3a.
   A. Of God
   B. Promised afore through his prophets in the holy scriptures

III. It concerns His Son, vs. 3b-5a.
   A. Of the seed of David according to the flesh
   B. Son of God as to the inner man
   C. Through Him we have received grace and apostleship

IV. It concerns those of Rome, vs. 5b-7.
   A. Among those who have obeyed the faith
   B. Called by Jesus Christ
   C. Beloved of God
   D. Called to be saints
   E. Recipients of grace and peace

It is easy to see the difference in outline. It would be possible to digress from the expository outline and not discuss the meaning and application of the text, thus destroying the real purpose of the expository outline. We assume you will not do this. Make all you preach relate directly to the text and its vital relationship to our lives.

Here are three outlines. Please read the text carefully and identify them as (1) *topical,* (2) *textual,* or (3) *expository.* Remember that the topical sermon obtains only its *theme* from the text. The textual sermon obtains the *theme, proposition,* and *main points* from the text.

(1) Text: Rom. 1:8-15
   Theme: Personal Desires of Paul
   Proposition: A consideration of Paul's desires

  I. He thanked God for the Christians at Rome, vs. 8.
    A. He thanked God for *everyone* of the Christians in the Roman church.
    B. Because of their "proclaimed" faith

 II. He longed to see the saints, vs. 11-12.
    A. That he might impart some spiritual gift
    B. That he might be comforted in them

III. He must pay his debt, vs. 13-15.
    A. He oftimes attempted to pay.
    B. He paid it in other Gentiles.
    C. He felt a compulsion to pay.
    D. He was ready to pay with all he had—to preach the gospel with his whole heart and mind.

Conclusion:

(2) Text: Rom. 1:8-15
   Theme: Personal Desires of Paul
   Proposition: Consideration of Paul's Desires

  I. Thanks for others
    A. This indicates unselfishness.
    B. This indicates godliness.
    C. This indicates Christ-likeness.

 II. Prayer for others
    A. For their fruitfulness
    B. For their protection
    C. For their unity

III. Preach to others
    A. This he did do.

B. This he must do.

C. This he chose to do.

Conclusion:

(3) Text: Rom. 1:8-15

Theme: Paul's personal desires

Proposition: Characteristics of these desires

I. Always for good of others
    A. With the Corinthians
    B. With the Ephesians
    C. With the Philippians

II. Always for the Gospel's sake
    A. That they would preach it
    B. That they would live it
    C. That they would defend it

III. Always in love
    A. Believed all things
    B. Hoped all things
    C. Endured all things

Conclusion:

How to Formulate an Expository Outline

This is a discussion on how *you* can formulate an expository outline, not how *I* do it, but how *you* can.

Let's work one up from Romans 1:16-17.

1. Text: Rom. 1:16-17
2. What is the obvious *theme* of this text?

Choose one: (*the one* of the inspired writer)

1. Not ashamed
2. God's preacher

71

3. God's power for salvation
4. Good news
5. From faith unto faith
6. How to live by faith
7. Salvation for all

We hope you chose either 3 or number 4.

3. How shall we obtain a proposition for this outline?

There are just six things we can say about this theme.
This will come as a surprise to some not acquainted with the six principles of discussion. Here they are; consider them carefully.

1. *What* - or the *characteristics* of the subject. In this we discuss its essential qualities or attributes.
2. *Why* - *Reasons.* This is a discussion of cause.
3. *How* - the principle of *method*
4. *Who* - a discussion of the *person* involved
5. *Where* - the *position* of the person or objects
6. *When* - the *time* element

When we have considered the ramifications of these six principles we have exhausted the subject.

Apply one or more of the six principles to the theme chosen. What is the theme? *God's power for salvation.*

Shall we discuss the *characteristics* or *attributes* of it? The proposition would then read, "Characteristics of the gospel (or God's power for salvation)." If we wanted to discuss the *reasons* or *causes,* the proposition would be, "Reasons for the gospel (or God's power for salvation)."

You form two more propositions using the principles of *How - Methods* and *Who - Persons.* They would appear as:

72

1. _____

2. _____

If we had a proposition such as "Some places where the power of God unto salvation is seen," which principles would be used?

Supposing the proposition was "Times for the power of God unto salvation." What is the obvious principle used?

4. We next need main divisions for this proposition. Please, please attempt to use the principle or principles (for more than one principle can and often times does appear in the proposition) the Holy Spirit used. Which one did the inspired writer use? Did he discuss the reasons? Characteristics? Persons? The answer to this will insure an expository development. Your main divisions can be those of the inspired writer *if* your principle of discussion is the same as the inspired writer.

See if you agree with this proposition as a possible expository expression of the inspired writer.

Proposition: "Persons involved in God's power unto salvation."

Then consider these main divisions as an expression or development of the proposition.

I.   The wise
II.   The foolish
III. The Greek
IV. The barbarian

Perhaps you feel that the last two are repetitious, and you used but two. After all, are not the wise and the Greek the same and the foolish and the barbarian? Perhaps. This is for you to decide in the light of the total context.

73

5. The next step is securing subdivisions for the main divisions. There is a definable method for doing this. Simply stated it is: *allow the main divisions to act as themes. Apply one or more of the six principles to them.* This will form a sub-proposition. Your development would look something like this:

I. The wise

  Sub-proposition: Reasons the wise need the gospel

The answers to your sub-proposition form your subdivisions. What are the reasons the wise need the gospel? Please make the reasons Paul's reasons. Perhaps they would read.

  A. Because they in their wisdom know not God
  B. Because their wisdom is not sufficient here or hereafter
  C. Because they are not truly wise

Would you please attempt a development of the second main division? Here it is: work out the sub-proposition and the subdivisions.

II. The foolish

  Sub-proposition: _____

  A. _____
  B. _____
  C. _____

So far we have worked from the text through the theme, proposition, main divisions to the subdivisions. This yet leaves the development of the conclusion.

See if you can develop an expository outline from the text, Romans 1:18-32. Perhaps the theme would be "The need of the Gospel among Gentiles." Form a complete outline.

How to Develop the Expository Outline

Essentially this is asking, "How shall we verbally support our sub-divisions?" To insure some order in answering this question, shall we produce an outline from Romans 1:18-32?

Text: Rom. 1:18-32
Theme: The need of the Gospel among the Gentiles
Proposition: Some reasons for the need of the gospel among the Gentiles.

I. Because they stifled the truth, v. 18-23
Sub-proposition: Methods of stifling the truth
  A. Through or by unrighteousness, v. 18b
  B. Through willful ignorance, v. 19-21
  C. Through vain profession of wisdom, v. 22-23

II. Because of immorality, v. 24-27
Sub-proposition: Characteristics of this immorality
  A. Unclean, v. 24a
  B. Bodies dishonored, v. 24b
  C. Service to the creature rather than the Creator, v. 25
  D. Homosexuality, v. 26-27

III. Because of intellectual dishonesty, v. 28-32
Sub-proposition: Results of such intellectual dishonesty
  A. Reprobate mind, v. 28
  B. Full of sin, v. 29-31
  C. Aggressive rejection, even to encouraging others to sin, v. 32

Conclusion:

With the outline before us, we should say there are at least seven ways of verbally supporting any point. These

75

can be found in variations in a great number of speech books.

1. Explanation
2. Illustration (hypothetical or real)
3. Analogy and comparison
4. Specific instance
5. Statistics
6. Testimony
7. Restatement

We shall illustrate the use of these seven forms of verbal support through the outline, but before we do we need to establish the purpose of our preaching. What do we hope to accomplish by way of application of the material? We believe the Holy Scripture has already set forth the purpose. We refer to II Timothy 4:2: "reprove, rebuke, exhort." Please define these words.

Reprove - "bring to the proof." We might say to offer evidence for acceptance. Someone made an assertion. Someone else said, "Prove it." This is the meaning of the word as here used by Paul. We could well say, "Prove it and then prove it again or *re-prove* it." We are well aware that the English word reprove is used in another sense, but we are concerned in its use in the purpose of preaching as stated in II Timothy 4:2.

Rebuke - This is the application word. Apply the truth to life. Relate your conduct, your words to God's word. The response you feel in your conscience is the rebuke of God. The preacher is to so specifically relate his material to the conduct of his hearers that they will believe God is speaking to their needs in a most personal manner.

Exhort - Of all the shortcomings of the preacher, this is surely the most obvious. We simply fail to move men to action. This is the action word. It might be a source of comfort as well as judgment, but by exhortation we are moved to acknowledge it or receive it. Incite or prompt to action, to preach for a verdict—this is our ultimate purpose in preaching.

All of our verbal support will be directed to accomplish one or more of these three divine purposes. Such verbal support should be delivered with all urgency at all times.

Now let's attempt the development of one of the subdivisions. Remember the outline? Here it is:

Text: Rom. 1:18-32
Theme: The need of the Gospel among the Gentiles
Proposition: Some reasons for the need of the Gospel among the Gentiles

I. Because they stifled the truth
   Sub-proposition: Methods of stifling the truth
   A. Through unrighteousness

(1) It is our task right here to verbally support this point in one or more of the seven ways we have indicated. Shall we *explain* how the truth is stifled through unrighteousness; i.e., shall we show the philosophical and psychological factors involved? If we choose this form of verbal support, we have chosen the first of the seven, *explanation.* This is a good method if we are careful with our use of words to make them incisive and penetrating in thought.

(2) Shall we choose to illustrate by *example* (preferably a biblical example) how unrighteousness stifles truth? Demas, who forsook the truth of the gospel and the apostle Paul because of his love of this present world, might offer an example. This is the second of the seven ways to support your point.

(3) An *analogy* or *comparison* is another form of illustration. It is more extended in form and analytical in use. A story could be told and the analogy left to the listener, but in the use of analogy and comparison, the comparative points of the story must be mentioned and emphasized. To develop by this means of verbal support we would obtain a story or incident in which a comparison could be made to prove by the points of comparison that unrighteousness stifles truth. We are *not* suggesting that the story or incident describes the stifling of truth by unrighteousness, but rather that the stifling of truth by unrighteousness is *just like* the incident used. Perhaps suffocation or asphyxiation could be made analogous to stifling truth through unrighteousness. A jilted lover and deacon in the church, who is also a filling station attendant drives his car into the garage of the station. He shuts all the doors, leaves the motor running, sits in the car, and falls asleep, never to awaken in this world. What are the analogous points in this story? Here are a few; you can think of others.

1. He knew the truth.	1. Gentiles in Paul's day knew the truth.
2. It is wrong to take life, yours or anothers.	2. Sin is defined or known by Gentiles, and by men today.
3. There is a stifling influence in carbon-monoxide.	3. All sin will have this influence or effect.
4. One sin leads to another, all the effect of clouding and stifling the judgment.	4. One rebellion and refusal of God's will leads to another, and all of them to a stifling of the truth.

78

5. No one knows how near to this tragic decision he or she might be.

5. None of us knows how near to stifling the truth our unrighteousness has brought us. Shall we repent of it or continue in it?

4. A *specific instance* is actually a shorter form of an illustration. We are dealing in concise examples. How many such examples can you produce of truth stifled by unrighteousness? The power of this verbal support is in the accumulation of very pointed examples. Please note the term *specific* instances. Can you show by ten instances that truth is stifled by unrighteousness? This is a very convincing verbal support.

5. *Statistics:* "Figures do not lie." This old cliche confirms the fact that people do accept the force of figures. How could we use statistics to prove truth is stifled by unrighteousness? How many perished in the flood because every imagination of their heart was evil continually? How many died in the fiery furnace of Sodom and Gomorrah because of their rejection of God's truth? We cannot give the exact number, but we can use the fact that great numbers were involved to verbally support the point.

6. *Testimony:* This form of verbal support must be given in the first person. We take the place of the person speaking and give his or her testimony concerning the point being made. This form adds the human element and human involvement. We all want to hear first hand what a person experienced. Using biblical examples in this form becomes a living Bible education.

7. *Restatement:* This is only used when we have used two or more of the other six forms of verbal support. Please

do not simply repeat in the same words what you said before. Offer variety of expression—repeat but do not become monotonous.

Note please the territory traversed thus far in our discussion of verbally supporting our points.

1. We have designated the seven ways a point could be supported and developed.
2. We suggested (but have not detailed) the three purposes in applying the material.

We want to say right here that all material will fall into one or another of these three purposes. We are either:

1. Proving a point (reprove)
2. Applying the material (rebuke)
3. Calling for a response (exhort)

Please consciously use such divine purposes in developing your sub-divisions.

We now want to suggest the third and last point in development. *We must have motives to which we appeal in our preaching.* Here are a list of ten; perhaps you can think of others.

1. Love
2. Courage
3. Pity
4. Beauty
5. Grace
6. Fear
7. Hope
8. Security
9. Reward
10. Holiness

When developing the subdivision that (1) Unrighteousness stifles truth, you do it through one of the seven forms of verbal support. You are either proving it, applying it, or calling for response to it. You now prove it, apply it, or exhort through one or more of the motives listed here.

Does this seem complicated? It shouldn't. Every sermon worthy of the name uses such development. We shall illustrate the material with one subdivision and then ask you to do it with the next one.

I. Because they stifled the truth
   Sub-proposition: Methods of stifling the truth
   A. Through unrighteousness

How to Illustrate an Expository Sermon

What is so different about illustrating an expository sermon from illustrating any other sermon? We might say "nothing" and dispense with the subject, but there *is* a difference. Shall we look into it?

Consider this expository outline:

Text: Romans 2:1-16
Theme: God's judgment
Propositon: Characteristics of God's judgment

I. According to truth, vs. 2
   Sub-proposition: Characteristics of God's truth as a basis for judgment.
   A. Revealed or knowledgeable truth

We now must decide if we are going to *support* this point (reprove), *apply* it (rebuke), or *call for action* upon it (exhort).

It would seem that such a subdivision needs proof or demonstration. To what *motive* shall we appeal in our proof? Would honesty or an appeal to the sense of fairness

81

be a good choice? Surely the subject matter would lend itself to such a motive.

Please notice here: *the use of illustration becomes a part of verbal support, however, the subdivision is used, i.e., in reprove, rebuke, or exhort, with whatever motive is used.*

Shall we say we have chosen to verbally support the subdivision with testimony? Consider the subdivision and its illustrative qualities:

I. God's judgment is according to truth.
   Sub-proposition: Characteristics of this truth
   A. It is revealed or knowledgeable truth.

We are to re-prove this thought, with the use of testimony with an appeal to the motive of honesty. We are now assuming the need for an illustration in the midst of this development.

By this time the reader should be able to see how very distinctive and selective the illustration must be to be usable in the expository sermon. But there are several types of illustration. Which one shall we use?

1. The story?
2. Parable?
3. Allegory?
4. Drama?
5. Object lesson?
6. Poem?
7. Quotation?
8. Simile?
9. Metaphor?
10. Hyperbole?

THE PESSIMIST TAKES THE CURE!

By Don H. Sharp

A. Pessimism is the inclination to put the least favorable construction upon anything that happens or may happen. A pessimist is one who sees
　1. Every traffic light as a stop light.
　2. And every silver-lined cloud as a thunderhead.
B. Of the twelve disciples, Thomas was the pessimist.
　1. When Jesus told his followers that Lazazrus was dead and that he was going to Bethany, you will remember that it was Thomas who pessimistically remarked, "Let us also go, that we may die with him."
　2. Later, when Jesus was telling His disciples that He was going to prepare a place for them, that where He was they might be also, you will remember it was old pessimistic Thomas who said, "Lord, we know not whither thou goest; how know we the way?"
　3. Finally, after our Lord's death and resurrection, it was Thomas who couldn't believe. Hearing the other disciples excitedly report of having seen the resurrected Lord, it was he who cried out, "Except I shall see in his hands the print of the nails, and put my finger into the print of the nails, and put my hand into his side, I will not believe."
C. Poor, poor Thomas. . .
　1. He had no faith in the mission of the Lord.
　2. No vision as to where the Lord could lead him.
　3. And no hope of ever seeing Jesus alive and well.
D. I can assure you Thomas was not the last of the

83

pessimistic disciples. He has his modern counter-parts. Counterparts who like Thomas

1. Have little or no faith in the mission of the Lord.
2. Or who have little or no vision as to where the Lord can lead them.
3. Or who have little or no hope of ever seeing Jesus alive and reigning as the King of Glory.

E. As a result of this pessimism, the pessimist,
1. Looks within himself and thus becomes de-pressed.
2. He looks behind and seeing all that has hap-pened, he becomes discouraged.
3. He then looks ahead and seeing the bleakness of food and energy shortages, environmental pollution and the system of Communism's world conquest, he becomes dismayed.

F. Let me tell you something—God didn't create us to live depressed, discouraged and dismayed. God came in Jesus Christ that in Him all of us might have hope:
1. Hope in a mission which transcends all missions.
2. Hope in a vision of what can be done when men have faith in the power of Christ to save us from our wickedness and weakness.
3. Hope in a life that has not been slammed down and riveted shut by the power of death.

G. Sometime ago, depressed over something that had happened, I found myself indulging in pessi-mistic attitudes. I was discouraged and dismayed and was enjoying it to the fullest, (Pessimism is enjoyable because it is an excuse not to attempt anything.) when across the way, from a school

84

yard I heard some children singing an old familiar
tune—"Farmer Takes A Wife." The joy of children at play soon had me thinking more positively
and I found myself singing "The pessimist takes
a cure, etc." But how? How can pessimistic Christians be cured of their pessimism?

Discussion

I. The Pessimist Takes the Cure By Meeting With The
   Disciples!
   A. John, in his gospel, tells us the extent of Thomas'
      depression and discouragement. When Christ
      appeared to His disciples on the evening of the day
      He arose—Thomas was not among them. For
      some unknown reason he had chosen to go it
      alone. His depression must have been intense, his
      discouragement complete. His response to their
      witness of having seen the Lord alive was one of
      total despondency. In his pessimism Thomas was
      convinced that following Jesus was a lost cause.
      He was dead and that was it. Finis! The End!
      1. A lot of disciples since Thomas have let pes-
         simism rob them of some great *discoveries*.
         Allowing themselves to put the least favorable
         construction of events they have become pessi-
         mistic in anything good ever coming out of
         following Jesus. Indulging themselves in their
         discouragement they have dropped out, con-
         vincing themselves that a crucified Christ is too
         weak to confront the powers and principalities
         of evil and its forces.

85

2. Like Thomas, they, when confronted with the witness of other disciples that Christ is alive, they disbelieve and cry out, "Except I shall see in his hands the print of the nails, and put my finger into the print of the nails, and put my hand into his side, I *will not* believe."

   a. I believe Thomas enjoyed his depression because it excused him from having to do anything about the awful state to which the world had come.

   b. I believe, too, a lot of hand-wringing Christians have come to the place that they enjoy their depression. It somehow, at least in their minds, excuses them from having to do anything about the sorry state to which our world has come.

3. There was something, however, that the pessimistic Thomas could not shake and that was the excited testimony of the other disciples who were reporting that something spectacular had happened on that very evening when he had chosen not to meet with them. Jesus had come! He is not dead but alive! "We have seen the Lord," they cried.

B. Thomas could have stayed away forever, lamenting what the world had come to, but he didn't. The next Sunday he met with the disciples and it happened again. Jesus appeared through shut doors and after greeting them all He spoke directly to Thomas. "Push hither thy finger, and see my hands; and reach hither thy hand, and put it into my side: and be not faithless, but believing." Thomas, the pessimist, found himself face to face with Him who had come to the world and as a result Thomas utters for all time the most profound statement, as to the identity of Christ, ever made. He says, "My Lord and my God."

C. It was not until Thomas met again with the disciples that anything happened to persuade him that all was not lost. A positive step for anyone wanting to rid themselves of their pessimism is to put oneself where Christ promised He would be.

1. Christ said, "Where two or three are gathered together in my name, there am I in the midst of them."

2. It was important for Thomas, and for us, not to stay away from the meeting of the disciples. Although all of us are but sinners saved by grace, it is in this company of the redeemed Jesus has chosen to reveal Himself and His will to those who will believe that Christ is alive and well!

II. The Pessimist Takes The Cure By Having Eyes to See Where the Lord Can Lead!

A. Jesus told Thomas, "Because thou hast seen me, thou hast believed: blessed are they that have not seen, and yet have believed." None of us have seen the Lord but we have believed nevertheless. In believing, God has given us a vision not common to man in general. God has given us a vision of what society could be if all men would become followers of Jesus Christ and walk as He walked.

1. That which is false, misleading, fake and deceitful will have passed away because the

87

followers of Christ will have put it away that they may speak truth each one with his neighbor.

2. Crime will have come to a screeching halt because he that stole will steal no more, but will instead work with his hands the thing that is good, that he may have whereof to give to him that hath need.

3. The scandalous literature of pornographic films will have ended; along with the cursing erupting out of the mouths of the young and old because men will feel the need for writing and speaking only that which edifies and builds up.

4. Wars will have ceased because the bitterness, wrath, anger, clamor and rioting will have been put away and men will have substituted kindness, tenderheartedness and forgiveness for all that malice which once ruled their lives.

B. Some, no doubt, at this point are shaking your heads in protest. "It will never be!" You cry out— man is too weak and wicked to put away his fakery, his greed, his lusts and hate for all those beautiful ideals of truth, honesty, purity and love and that's just the point—the wicked and the weak, by some dark law, have a strange power to shut and rivet down their own horizons round us, to unwing our heaven-aspiring visions.

C. We must refuse to let them do this. We must break out of this pessimism and let our faith in Christ show us what it could be like if we begin walking even as he walked.

1. Prov. 29:18 says, "Where there is no vision, the people perish." And that is true—they are eaten up in lies, inundated in crime, overwhelmed

88

in corruption, and ripped apart, burned up and ravaged in war.

2. A vision foretells what may be ours. It is an invitation to do something. With a great mental picture in mind we go from one victory to another, using the materials about us only as stepping stones to that which is higher, and nobler, and better. In the process we become possessors of the unseen values which are eternal. We become citizens of that Holy City whose builder and maker is God.

D. I have a vision and it's no little one. It is a vision of many of us, right here, putting away that old way of living which was rotten through and through with lusts' illusion and putting on the new way of living which is our believing that we can do all things through Him that strengtheneth us.

1. It may not change the world but it can make the little corner of which we are a part a better place to live.

2. It may not significantly change the city in which we live but it will deliver some of us from our pessimism and put us in position to accomplish that which we could never have accomplished had we not been set free to *do something*.

E. Jesus told Thomas, "Because thou hast seen me, thou hast believed: blessed are they that have not seen, and yet have believed." I haven't seen Jesus but because of Him I have a vision that foretells what someday will be ours.

III. The Pessimist Takes the Cure by Believing Again In the Mission of the Lord!

89

A. It is written in John 3:16 that God so loved the world, he gave his only begotten Son that whosoever believeth on Him should not perish but have everlasting life. Christ's mission was to save us.
   1. From ignorance!
   2. From our own demented self-interest!
   3. From sin!
   4. From the influence of this present evil world!
   5. And from Satan and his power of death!
B. Christ's mission *has not* changed. To listen to some people talk you would think that it is all over. That we are, somehow, a lost cause on our way to Jerusalem to be crucified. Like Thomas' old begrudging lament some are saying, "Let us go and die with him."
   1. I say to hell with this kind of defeatism. The mission of Christ is not finished, nor will it be until He comes again in power and glory.
   2. Christ is the same yesterday, today and forever. He came to save that which was lost and that mission is just as valid today as it was 2,000 years ago—more so—for we are nearer to salvation than when we first believed.
C. Let us be done with the idea that Christ's mission has somehow lost its thrust. If there ever were a time for faith in the mission of our Lord it is now.
   1. Now when the power of spiritual ignorance darkens the mind of so many.
   2. Now when self-interest is so prevalent and so attractively presented.
   3. Now when sin rages like a consuming fire on the verge of being out of control.

      4. Now when evil's influence appears to be ready to declare itself to be the absolute master of the minds, hearts, and bodies of men.

      5. Now when Satan and his power of death seems so close to victory.

D. Now is the time for a new determination, not to trudge along with Jesus that we might die with Him, but that we might march with Him to live with Him and to share with Him the victory God will surely give Him!

Conclusion

A. Thomas was not the last of the pessimistic disciples—each age has had its own; pessimists who

      1. Have little or no faith in the mission of the Lord.

      2. Or who have little or no vision of where the Lord is leading them.

      3. Or who have little or no hope of ever seeing Jesus alive and reigning as King of Glory.

B. Our age is not without its pessimists. They are all over the place.

      1. Looking within they are depressed.

      2. Looking behind they are discouraged.

      3. Looking ahead they are dismayed.

C. Enough is enough! The resurrection of Christ is positive proof that God is not through with us yet. Christ is not dead but alive!

      1. The time is coming when we shall see Him, full of grace and truth. Remember it was he who said, "Behold I come quickly: hold that fast which thou hast, that no man take thy crown" (Rev. 3:11).

2. The time is coming and now is, when we must refuse to let the wicked and weak to shut and rivet down our horizons with their own. We must develop a vision of what it all could be like if we would all walk even as He walked. Such a vision is an invitation to do great things!

3. The time is long past that we Christians believe again in the mission of our Lord and not only believe but act on that commission which Christ commissioned us to do; i.e., to go and preach and teach and baptize that all nations might become His disciples, His promise is, that, if we observe whatsoever He commanded us, He in turn, will be with us even unto the end of the world. Don't you see why it is important to meet with the disciples—it is there where Christ is—among those meeting in His name and doing what He commanded.

THE GOSPEL OF CHRIST
Romans 1:16, 17

By Sam E. Stone

Introduction

Not long before he was killed in a plane crash several years ago, Mr. Dag Hammarkskjold was visited by Billy Graham in his office at the United Nations. The famous evangelist reports that the U. N. Secretary General seemed deeply distressed during their conversation.

Looking from his window across New York, the world leader declared, "I see no hope for permanent world peace. We have tried so hard, we have failed so miserably." Then he paused a moment, looked at the evangelist, and said, "Unless the world has a spiritual rebirth within the next few years, civilization is doomed."

The problem of war is still with us. The problems of our universe are compounded. The cause of these problems still has not been dealt with—sin in the human heart. There is only one solution to this problem: the gospel of Jesus Christ.

This is the theme of the book of Romans. Romans has been called the finest exposition of the gospel in print. The text gives the central idea of the entire book. This is the essence of Paul's message (*read Romans 1:16 and 17*). We learn three things about the gospel of Christ in these lines:

All Powerful

It is all powerful because "it is the power of God." He alone is omnipotent. Because Paul's message did not have a human source, he could say and mean, "I am not ashamed of it." What Rome meant to that ancient world is almost beyond our comprehension. We must imagine it as all the modern capital cities together—Washington, Paris, London, Moscow, Tokyo, Peking, all in one. See in contrast the itinerant preacher, Paul, who is setting out to conquer Rome for Christ with the power of the gospel.

What does he mean "power"? The very name "Rome" meant power. The greatest army, the finest government, the most powerful laws.

"Oh, no," says Paul, "that is not power at all." The power of the gospel is so much greater that it cannot even be compared with frail boasts of human strength. The gospel is great and our message is mighty, not because of polished preachers, entertaining evangelists, witty writers, or sophisticated scholars. All of its strength is due to its source—it comes from God.

The gospel is God's *power*. All of us have heard that the word for power used in the original is that from which we get "dynamite." This suggests great force. And the gospel has it! Few things really change men. Marriage can. One fellow remarked that his friend's wedding ring must fit pretty tight because it certainly had cut down his circulation! When you mean your wedding vows, they will change your life. But the gospel is even greater. It unites you to Christ—not "til death do you part"—but even beyond the grave. It brings a changeless relationship that goes through all eternity. This is God's *power*, and we should also emphasize that it is God's *power*, not ours. The gospel is all powerful.

All Effective

The gospel is effective. It is *unto salvation*. It works. It is as advertised. It is guaranteed if you follow directions

(II Corinthians 10:4, 5). Look at the life of the writer. Paul had been a bitter enemy of the church; he persecuted it with fanatic zeal. He tried to kill every Christian. If ever there were one who was completely against the gospel of Christ, it would be Saul of Tarsus.

But he changed. And he changed because of the gospel. True, he had a miraculous vision of Christ that we do not expect to receive, but this is not the point. We find he became a Christian in the very way that men today must. It was not the blinding light on the road that saved him; it was not the experience of a personal encounter with Christ that saved him; it was not the prayer and fasting for three days that saved him. We know this for certain for when he had been there in Damascus, God sent a man (a preacher) to him. The man said, "And now, Saul, why tarriest thou, rise and be baptized and wash away thy sins calling on the name of the Lord" (Acts 22:16).

It was the gospel that brought salvation to Saul. The same gospel can bring it for your life. You need Jesus too. You may not have persecuted the church, but you have turned your back on God's will and way. Like the prodigal son, you've lost your inheritance. You need to return to the Father in repentance.

Verse 17 adds: "For in it the righteousness of God is revealed from faith to faith; as it is written, but the righteous man shall live by faith." Through the gospel we received faith; by the gospel we live in faith. When we accept it, our lives change.

An atheist on a South Pacific island some years ago was talking with the native chief about the Bible. He laughed when the chief said that he believed it. "It's a good thing for you that I do," the chief replied.

"What do you mean?" the man asked.

"Simply this. If we had not been taught to believe all the things in the Bible, we'd still be cannibals. You'd look like a good meal for a hungry man!"

The gospel of Christ, however, changes a man. It is the power of God unto salvation. The verse concludes that it is also,

To All Men

The gospel of Christ is God's power " to *everyone* that believeth." Paul told the Corinthians this (I Corinthians 1:18). First it was preached to the Jews (Acts 2) and then later to the Greeks (See Acts 13:46). Basil Holt has observed that if one combines Colossians 3:11 and Galatians 3:28 the equality of the gospel is outlined completely:

Neither Greek nor Jews (no political separation)

No circumcision nor uncircumcision (no ecclesiastical separation)

No barbarian nor Cythian (no intellectual separation)

No bond nor free (no social separation)

No male nor female (no sexual separation).

All are one in Christ Jesus. The gospel is for everyone.

But not really *everyone*. There is this limiting qualification. "To everyone that believeth." God *wants* to save all men, but some won't be saved because they refuse to believe and obey God's message. Jesus promised, "he that believeth and is baptized, shall be saved" (Mark 16:16). Every man may come to Christ, but only those who *do* come can be saved.

A short time after the Battle of Waterloo in which the Duke of Wellington defeated Napoleon, the Duke came to a communion service. Upon seeing who he was, the priest asked the other worshipers to leave. The Duke beckoned for them to stay. "Here," he said, "all men are equal."

The ground is level at the foot of the cross. Everyone in the community needs the gospel. God is able and willing to save everyone who turns to Him. The burning question concerns your relationship to God. Have you believed the gospel? Have you accepted His Son? Are you living in His will? Do you serve Him in His church, awaiting His return? You may have problems, questions, doubts. Bring them to Jesus. He can help you. He can solve them. He can save you and He alone.

THE GRACE OF GOD HATH APPEARED
Titus 2:11-14

By Orval M. Morgan

The grace of God hath appeared! What an announcement! What good news for fallen man! For the Jew, the Messiah is announced; for the Gentile, a Saviour has come. In these few verses we have John 3:16 restated and explained. Here is the epitome of the Gospel of Christ, showing its origin, its end, its benefactors and its divine method couched in the language of Paul as directed by the Holy Spirit. Certainly such a summation of divine truth is worthy of our study and understanding.

Let us then consider the revealed truth that God has made known, His divine plan for the salvation of all men.

The divine truth is announced.

In the opening statement, we find four truths upon which all the rest is based. The understanding of these is important if we are to fully comprehend what follows. The first truth is "The grace of God." We are introduced to the doctrine of grace versus works. Man was not, and is not now, able to come up with a plan to redeem mankind from his sin. The world calls it "foolishness" but those being saved, call it God's power and God's grace. John 1:17 says that "the law came through Moses, grace and truth came through Jesus Christ." Paul tells us in Ephesians 2:8 that "For by grace have ye been saved through faith; and that not of yourselves, it is the gift of God." God, the One sinned against from the beginning, prepared and sent His grace gift in His Son. It is His favor we enjoy, and we could say with Simeon of old (Luke 2:30-32) "For mine eyes have seen thy salvation which thou hast prepared before the face of all peoples; a light for revelation to the Gentiles, and the glory of thy people Israel."

98

But God's grace is not something lately invented. God has been most gracious from the beginning. The difference now is that it has appeared in definite form, "making known to us the mystery of his will, according to his good pleasure which he purposed in him unto a dispensation of the fulness of the times,—in whom ye also, having heard the word of the truth, the gospel of your salvation,—in whom, having also believed, ye were sealed with the Holy Spirit of promise which is an earnest of our inheritance, unto the redemption of God's own possession, unto the praise of his glory" (Ephesians 1:9-14).

The same truth is given in Luke 2:1-14 when the birth of Christ was announced—"for there is born to you this day in the city of David a Saviour, Christ the Lord." God's grace hath appeared!

If God had manifested His grace in days gone by, and He had, what makes this so different? The difference is found in what this grace brought from heaven. No longer will it be the rolling back of sins, the offering of sacrifices, and the keeping of feast days, for this grace has brought salvation. What a word! What does it mean? It means something of what the father said in the parable of the lost boy,—"for this thy brother was dead, and is alive again; was lost and is found" (Luke 15:32). The long awaited Messiah has come. Salvation spoken of by Christ during his earthly ministry as being near, has arrived. Lost man can now be saved. The grave is not the end, faith turns to knowledge and hope to fruition as salvation appears. This is the good news of God, announced, demonstrated, and attested. This grace that appeared—the Good News in Christ—becomes "the power of God unto salvation to everyone that believeth" (Rom. 1:16). Christ had told his followers that His mission was to "seek and to save that which is lost" (Luke 19:10) and now it has become a fact.

But without this last truth, it would be tragic. All of this wonderful revelation is for "all men." No longer Jew and Gentile; bond and free; male or female, but all men everywhere had made available to them the salvation of God's grace. Here John 3:16 is restated in a short statement. Whosoever will becomes more than just rhetoric, it is another manifestation of God's grace.

In this verse then we have an epitome of the Gospel. With the supporting revelation of the Word, all men are called upon to examine the evidence and BELIEVE "that God is and is a rewarder of them that diligently seek him" (Hebrews 11:6) and knowing that he is "encompassed about with so great a cloud of witnesses" (Hebrews 12:1a) he is urged to follow the divine instructions unto perfection and eternal salvation.

Instructions are given that will assure the proper and intended results.

If faith alone could save, we would not need the verses that follow verse eleven. But the revealed fact that God's grace has appeared, does not signify that all men will accept it. Man is saved by grace through faith as we have learned. He must have an active faith like we find in Hebrews, chapter 11. Every time faith is mentioned, it is followed by an active verb. So our faith must result in action, the kind of action that will produce divine results. The action called for is logical and sensible. It follows the divinely ordained process as is illustrated in the Acts of the Apostles. Our text says, "instructing us to the intent"—(or for the purpose of)—(v. 12a). What does this mean? What instruction do we have? What is the purpose of such?

100

It simply means that man must appropriate God's means of salvation. He must do something about it. But not knowing what to do nor how, he must be instructed. Do we have the instructions? Yes. In Acts 2:42 we find the early Christians continuing in the Apostles' doctrine. Ever wonder why they did? It was God's instruction manual. As Paul tells Timothy (II Timothy 3:15) "and that from a babe thou hast known the sacred writings which are able to make thee wise unto salvation through faith which is in Christ Jesus."

Jesus said, "Ye shall know the truth and the truth shall make you free" (John 8:32). In the divine revelation we have the truth which will make man free and such is the purpose of the instruction. But what are the definite instructions alluded to in this passage?

We find they are twofold—"denying" and "living." Let us look at these for a moment. What is meant by denying as used here? Perhaps we could use the word "unlearn." The word "repent" fits also. Is it easy to unlearn? Ever try to break a habit? To correct mistakes in your English? These are or may be lesser things, but have you tried to repent and stop sinning? It becomes what Jesus was speaking about in Luke 9:32 when he said, "If any man would come after me, let him deny self and take up his cross and follow me." Or as the Hebrew letter states it, (Hebrews 12:1b) "lay aside every weight and the sin which doth so easily beset us." In other words this is plain simple repentance in its original meaning. I Thessalonians 1:9 gives a good definition. "How ye turned from idols to serve a living and true God" says Paul.

The two specific areas set forth in our text are quite inclusive. The first word is "ungodliness"—what does this

101

mean? Living without any recognition of God in ones life is ungodliness. Failing to recognize Him as a personal Saviour, Helper, Sovereign, Judge and the eternal sustainer of life falls into the same bracket. A short answer would be void of God and His control. The second word is equally important. It is "worldly lust." What is this? A passion for the things of the world which perish with the using and which never ennobles the soul. It could be the man Paul spoke of in Philippians 3:19 "whose end is perdition, whose God is the belly, and whose glory is in their shame, who mind earthly things."

To summarize these we could say that salvation includes the putting away of every thought, act, and word which excludes God and debases our character. This is indeed a turning, a repentance which includes a sense of sin, a sorrow for sin and a severance from sin.

We come now to the positive side where the word is "LIVE." This is what it is all about. The Christian life is an activity not a form nor description of something. In His discourse on Life in John 6:52-56, we get a picture of His concept of Life. That which He came to give and make abundant can only be enjoyed when the soul has been turned around, cleansed and motivated. Hebrews 12:1c indicates that we are to "run with patience the race that is set before us, looking unto Jesus." However in so doing our text points out three areas to be found in this activity. They are "soberly," "righteously," and "godly." Let us examine these three aspects.

Soberly means self-control, temperate, well balanced, rationally, reasonably, seriously, with all abstinence, gravity and sobriety. This has to do with our duties to ourselves.

Righteously means pure, noble, upright, just, merciful, the showing of prudence, chastity, hitting the mark, and walking in the right path. This points up our conduct toward our fellow men.

Godly carries with it the ideas of reverence, devotion, holiness, I Peter 1:15-16. Such a one would be saintly, blameless, humble, spiritually minded, spirit filled, sanctified. He would stand up for his Christ, obey Him and love Him. This guides us in our duty to our God.

In doing these things a man would see the implementation of the Good Confession and the culminating action of Christian baptism which ultimates in a new creature in Christ Jesus. Before leaving this point, it would be well to note where this is all to take place. The writer says, "in this present world" which would indicate not only place but time. It is here and only here during our lifetime that this opportunity is offered. It is NOW that we are to act. II Corinthians 6:2b, "behold now is the acceptable time; behold, now is the day of salvation." Christ called His own the "light" and the "salt" of the world. Beginning in the act of baptism and continuing as admonished by Peter, II Peter 3:18, "But grow in the grace and knowledge of our Lord, and Saviour Jesus Christ," we become: "children of God without blemish in the midst of a crooked and perverse generation, among whom ye are seen as lights in the world holding forth the word of life," (Philippians 2:15).

The motive and goal are set forth.

Most of us know more than we do! Why? Largely because we lack motivation and a goal. To a ship without a port no wind is favorable. Christ gave us another reason when He said, "The spirit is willing, but the flesh is weak" (Matthew 26:41). The writer of Hebrews makes it plain when he says, "looking unto Jesus the author and perfector of our faith" (Hebrews 12:2). Yes, we have a battle at best, even as Paul expressed in the 7th of Romans. We must have something to lead us on. Perhaps it can be best expressed in two words, namely WORSHIP and WORK.

The motive and goal are closely knit in this passage, but looking carefully we can see them. We are commanded to be "looking for the blessed hope and appearing of the glory of the great God and our Saviour Jesus Christ," verse 13. So strong is this that Paul feels it necessary to tell us three of our Lord's supreme accomplishments. He says, He gave Himself for us; He redeemed us; and purified us to be His own. The impact of these truths should motivate any one of us. Think what has been done for us. Is this not grace indeed? In our worship about the table we remember this gracious act. "For as often as ye eat this bread and drink the cup, ye proclaim the Lord's death till he come" (I Corinthians 11:26). As redeemed, purified children of God, we have but one great desire, (Colossians 3:17) "And whatsoever ye do, in word or deed, do all in the name of the Lord Jesus, giving thanks to God the Father through him."

Yet there is more than just worship. Involved in this, for worship is a continuous action, is the work we must do. "Zealous of good works" the writer says (Ephesians 2:10). "For we are his workmanship, created in Christ Jesus for good works." There is work to do, a Gospel to be preached, a life to be lived, a heaven to be gained. The great commission gives us our orders for operation. The perfecting of our own lives must also be included, II Peter 1:5-11. Paul admonished the Philippian brethren to "Have this mind in you which was also in Christ Jesus," (2:5) and "work out your own salvation with fear and trembling" (2:12).

This does not imply nor suggest that these works accrue to our credit or glory, for such is not the case. In Luke 17:10 we find Christ's words—"Even so ye also, when ye shall have done all the things that are commanded you, say, We are unprofitable servants; we have done that which it was our duty to do." We must do His work even as Christ came and did the work of Him who sent Him. In all of Paul's letters we are admonished to do good works. How could any one stop us when we feel, see and experience the grace of God?

In the light of this great passage we see the divine truth which has been revealed, realizing the wonderful grace of God and the extent of its reach and the purpose for which it was given. We are made to know what is expected for us and the manner in which it is to be accomplished. And we are given a motive and a goal to lead us to the desired end. What does this mean to you and me? We are included in the "all men" phrase, and as recipients of this grace, so freely offered, we must make the supreme decision to accept it or reject it. God has done all He can and will do to save you and mankind. It is now up to you and others as to what will be done. The grace has appeared, the way has been opened, the eternal reward offered, what is your decision? Salvation is yours if you so decide. Can it be that His grace has appeared for naught? Can it be that even though some of you have accepted His grace that you are not actively working for Him, engaged in "good works"? You are asked to appraise your condition and do what you know needs to be done in your life to make this wonderful grace effective. "The grace of God hath appeared" —it is for you.

CHRIST'S CALL:
TO COMFORT OR COMMITMENT?

Matthew 11:28-30

By Douglas A. Dickey

Several months ago while sitting in a dentist's office I picked up a woman's magazine and read an article by a professional interior decorator. She was suggesting to women who wanted to do their own decorating, that they walk into the room to be done and look at it as though they had never seen it before. This new perspective on the problem would, according to the professional, stimulate the imagination so that new and creative ideas would come to mind.

It occurred to me that this suggestion could be used in our approach to the Bible. The old and familiar texts have little to say to us when our imagination has gone dead. Perhaps if we made the conscious effort to free ourselves from our habitual points of view, the Word might again speak to us in exciting and relevant ways.

The beautiful words of Matthew 11:28-30 are a case in point. We know that something wonderful and significant is being said here, but the very beauty of the words has served to obscure the power and practicality of what Jesus is saying to us. We may, for instance, fail to see the sharp paradox which is just under the surface of these familiar words. On the one hand, Jesus is calling us to be comforted, to have our burdens lifted. On the other hand he is urging upon us a yoke, a heavy load of responsibility. Depending upon our basic views of the essence of the Christian Gospel, we hear sharply contrasting messages from these well-known words. If we understand Christianity as primarily aimed at comforting us, as creating peace of mind, we hear Jesus' call to ease and relief from burdens. However, if we see the Gospel as urging upon us our duty to man and our obligations to God, we hear the call to responsibility, to increased effort. That these two radically different messages can be heard in the same passage has not often occurred to us.

Can we approach this text with enough imagination to resolve this paradox? What is Christ's call, is it to comfort, or to commitment?

The Call To Comfort.

The call to comfort is very attractive to modern men and women. Doctors say that the most frequent words they hear from their patients are, "I'm just tired all the time." There is much in comtemporary life to make us tired. Coping with the increasing complexity of day to day existence is in itself exhausting, not to mention the extra demands made upon us by family, job and social responsibilities. The promise of comfort, of an escape from daily routine and constant pressure, is a welcome one. It isn't only modern men who long for escape. Many biblical characters also looked for release from various kinds of pressure. There were those who ran away out of weakness, like Jonah running from God and Ninevah,

Demas deserting Paul in a crisis, and John Mark going home to mother from the rigors of missionary service in Asia Minor. But there were strong men who sought relief from responsibility also. Moses retreated to Midian from his duty in Egypt, Elijah ran to the broom tree, exhausted from his labors and frightened of Jesebel, and Jeremiah longed to retreat to the tranquility of the desert even while he prophesied in Jerusalem.

Jesus' call to comfort touches a deep need in us, a need for relief, for retreat, for rest from the rigors of life itself.

The Call To Commitment

Yet the call to commitment appeals to us also. There *are* burdens to be borne, work to be done, loads to be lifted. We hear Robert Frost when he says:

> The woods are lovely, dark and deep.
> But I have promises to keep,
> and miles to go before I sleep.[1]

Much has been made recently of the influence upon our contemporary culture of the "Puritan work ethic." It is probably true that influences from our stern Calvinistic forefathers have created an over-developed sense of responsibility in most Americans. And yet there is something deeper than our cultural conditioning that urges us to accept obligations and to assume duties.

A famous American educator once called a student into his office because the student had missed several days of classes. When the young man offered the excuse that he "wasn't feeling very well," the older man said, "Son, most

---

1. From poem by Robert Frost, "Stopping By the Woods On A Snowy Evening."

of the world's work is done by people who are not feeling very well." There is much absenteeism and escapism, but the world's work does get done, obligations are met, jobs are finished and promises are kept, because men and women need to carry burdens to feel like men and women.

Criticism of the Contrasting Calls

We need, however, to look more deeply into what Jesus is saying to us in this text. It is possible to be critical of both the call to comfort, and the call to commitment, when they are stated as we have suggested above.

When Christianity is understood *only* as an escape from burdens and responsibility, it creates false hopes which lead to disillusionment. If an appeal is made to people to turn to Christ because he will lead them into a tranquil and trouble-free existence they are headed for real trouble. If they do not become bitter and turn away from Christ entirely, they may try to live the illusion and become phoney and unreal. Both reactions are tragic consequences of hearing only the call to comfort.

Perhaps a more serious criticism of the "call-to-comfort-Christianity" is that it shifts responsibility for the condition of the world onto God. Although we Christians have been very defensive about it, both Karl Marx and Sigmund Freud saw this weakness in the distorted Christianity in their day. Marx called religion "the opiate of the people," and Freud saw it as an escape into illusion. Marx saw an orthodox church that had become rich and fat and totally unresponsive to the needs of people, and Freud dealt with sick and neurotic people who were trying to make religion an escape from responsibility and reality. Biblical warnings against this kind of misinterpreted message are loud and clear if we will hear them. Indeed the fatal flaw of God's chosen people under the old covenant was that they thought they were chosen to be comforted instead of to be committed. Hear Amos, speaking for God:

> I hate, I despise your feasts,
>   and I take no delight in your solemn assemblies.
> But let justice roll down like waters,
>   and righteousness like an ever-flowing stream
>   (Amos 5:21, 24).

But hearing only the call to commitment can lead to serious consequences also. People who understand Christianity *only* as urging upon them obligations and duties are subject to another kind of disillusionment—the kind that leads to despair. Ernest T. Campbell speaks of "mathematical religion" in which people try to reach God by addition, subtraction or multiplication. Some try to add to their lives certain actions or virtues which they hope will improve their standing with God. Still others try to achieve peace by subtracting from their lives certain undesirable habits or attitudes. But the deadliest of all the mathematical Christians are the multipliers. They are the activists who try to take on more responsibilities, attend more meetings, support more causes until they are emotionally and spiritually exhausted.

Dr. Campbell says:

> Unfortunately, the more sincere we are the more likely we are to be caught up in the quest for intensity. No minister who has been around for a decade or two will fail to recall people—who burned themselves out and then became angry with the institution that consumed their commitment.[2]

2. From a radio sermon by Ernest T. Campbell on "National Radio Pulpit," May-June 1974. Available in printed form from "National Radio Pulpit." Box 30, N.Y., N.Y. 10027

If we are rigorously honest with ourselves, we will admit that such people are often exploited by the church. They are used to keep the programs going and to build the institution, and then are discarded when the disillusionment sets in. Is it possible that we in the contemporary church deserve the devastating attack of Jesus upon the religious leaders of his day?

> They bind heavy burdens, hard to bear, and lay them on men's shoulders (Matthew 23:4).

Underlying the "call-to-commitment-Christianity" is the assumption that men are capable of carrying all the burdens of life, and taking complete responsibility for themselves. The roots of this attitude are pride and insipient spiritual rebellion which seeks to avoid humiliating dependency, even on God.

Reconciliation of the Conflicting Calls

That there is indeed a paradox in Jesus's teaching at this point should not dismay us. Paul Tillich has reminded us that truth often can be expressed only in paradox, not because it is illogical, but because it is too great to be expressed in only logical terms.[3]

I suggest that a clue to the message of this paradoxical passage may be found in the possibility that Jesus was here speaking out of his own experience. If, as is highly probable, Jesus did spend the greater part of the eighteen "silent years" of his life in the carpenter shop, then he knew about burdened animals and yokes.

Let us imagine that a farmer brought a sore and burdened beast to Jesus to have him reshape an ill-fitting yoke. With

---

3. Paul Tillich, "Systematic Theology" Vol. I, pp. 56, 57. The University of Chicago Press.

concerned tenderness he would remove the old yoke from the exhausted beast. He would treat the wounds, allow the animal to rest and recover, while a new yoke was shaped. There is a legend that over the carpenter shop in Nazareth was a sign, "My Yokes Are Easy." (The Greek word in the text means "well-fitting.")

With care and skill Jesus would measure, shape and carve a new yoke. Then, the beast having recovered, he would place the new yoke on its back, fitted now so that work could be done without galling and exhausting pain.

Such a use of our imagination can suggest some very profound meanings in this passage of scripture.

First, it reminds us that the Gospel begins with Jesus lifting our burdens. The fallacy of those who say that Christianity weakens men by removing their responsibilities is that they assume that man is capable of taking entire responsibility for himself. Some burdens are beyond man's capabilities. He cannot carry his guilt, for example. Like Cain he knows, consciously or sub-consciously, that his punishment is more than he can bear. He seeks relief in psychoanalysis, or in drugs, or in pleasure, or in rationalizations. But he cannot throw off the burden—it must be lifted from him by Someone who has the leverage to do so.

An even heavier weight is the burden of meaninglessness. Man may repress or project his guilt and deal with it, at least temporarily. But who is to tell him who he is and where he is going ultimately? Victor Frankl discovered in the concentration camps of Europe that men died, not because they were tortured or starved, but because they had no meaning for their lives.

The priorities are important here. Jesus does not come to us at first to lay obligations upon us. Society does, the church does, and we lay such burdens upon ourselves. But Jesus comes to those who are sick of obligations and failed responsibilities. He comes asking us to repent in the most profound of all ways, that is to change our mind about who we really are and to give up our attempts to live apart from God.

After he has lifted our burdens of guilt and meaninglessness, he will give us healing and renewal deep within us. Then he will shape and carve a yoke to put upon us, but now we can carry loads of responsibility because we have found the inner strength, the resources we previously lacked.

If we are correct in this understanding of this text, then it is a fatal misunderstanding of the nature of the Gospel to call men to commitment before they have understood themselves in relation to the gift of grace and acceptance. The whole context of our lives is changed when we give up our strenuous efforts to do something or become someone, and allow Jesus to lift the burdens of our self-centeredness.

The rest he speaks of is not temporary relief or neurotic escape, but a deep-seated awareness of one's acceptance by God. In this awareness one can take on burdens, but now the motivation for doing so is changed from duty to gratitude. A new focusing and selectivity comes into play, so that decisions can be made about which burdens to carry, and for what purpose.

Perhaps best of all is the knowledge of resources which are available to carry burdens. The yoke used in the ancient world was often a team yoke, for two beasts of burden working in tandem. Certainly the yoke Jesus puts upon us after we are healed and renewed, is a double yoke, and he is carrying the other half. He not only carries some of

113

the load, but he also takes some of the responsibility. We are freed from the exhausting effort of trying to do everything. He also grants to us the honor of helping him to carry some of his loads, to do his work in the world, guided by his insights and supported by his presence and power.

More times than I can count this message, so understood, has ministered to my deepest needs. There are times, and surely all men share this experience, when not only my responsibilities and duties, but life itself has become too much to bear. In such times of exhaustion and near-despair, I can consciously turn to Jesus, asking for relief and rest. I can do so, however knowning that he will honor me by giving back my obligations, but now in an entirely new perspective. I am refreshed by his forgiveness, the loads are fitted to my abilities, and I know that I am not ever alone in the struggle and adventure.

The German philosopher Schiller once told a parable of the day when the birds all walked the earth without wings. God came down to a little sparrow with a pair of wings. The sparrow rebelled. He could hardly walk as he was, with his little spindly legs. How could he carry all that extra load? But God was insistent, so finally, feeling very full of self-pity, the little sparrow put on the wings. He walked off, dragging the wing-tips in the dust. A day or two later he was able to lift them up and flap them a little. A few days more and he was able to jump up to the low branches of a bush. Then one memorable day, he flew off into the air, flying as birds are supposed to do. God does not want us to be burdenless, or overburdened, but he wants to give us the burdens that will enable us to live like the men and women he planned us to be in the first place.

A QUALITY COMMITMENT
Acts 21:17, 22:1-22

By E. Ray Jones

A modern novel begins with a career Navy man musing about his new assignment and the effect it will have on his marriage. The Commander says, "At 45 Rhoda remained a singularly attractive woman but she was rather a crab. This discolored her judgment and this was a fault he found hard to forgive. She had married him with her eyes wide open. They had talked frankly about the drawbacks of the military life, the separations, the lack of a real home, the need to be humble to senior men's wives. But Rhoda had declared that none of them would trouble her. She loved him and the Navy was a career of honor. So she said in 1915 when the World War was on and the the uniform had a glow. But this was 1939 and she had long since forgotten those words."

There was a day when in a flash of blinding light Saul of Tarsus met The Risen Lord. That moment, Saul, later renamed Paul, made a commitment of his life to this Lord. His words, "Lord, what will you have me to do?" were indicative of a desire for his life to take a new direction, a direction that would be dictated by God. There never was a time from that moment on when that commitment faltered. Over a period of many years all sorts of pressures were put on that initial commitment but it never collapsed.

The Scripture that forms the basis of our thinking today permits us to witness one of those situations where the commitment of this man of God was put to the test. The depth of the quality commitment evidenced in the life of the apostle Paul to the situation that faced him is an example, an inspiration and a guide line for the people of God in

115

all ages by which we can measure the quality of our commitment.

I. First this Scripture points out the necessity, if our commitment is to be a quality one, of our willingness to put into practice the principle of expediency. The Church at Jerusalem was facing a situation that demanded such expedient action. The Jewish Christians, even though they had accepted Christ, still maintained a strong attachment to the customs of the Old Testament, namely the circumcision of their children and the keeping of particular laws of purification. The rumor was being circulated that Paul was trying to persuade the Jews living among the Gentile nations to forsake those cherished customs. This was of course not true. Paul with his own hand had circumsized Timothy. He did so because the young man was going to work among the Jewish community and Paul felt that it was expedient that Timothy keep this Jewish custom.

The word expediency means "a means of achieving a particular end." Since the end the leaders of the Church at Jerusalem were trying to achieve was to put to rest these false rumors, the method they suggested, and with which Paul complied, was to practice this principal of expediency. Acts 21:23-26a, "Do therefore this that we say to thee: We have four men which have a vow on them; Them take, and purify thyself with them, and be at charges with them that they may shave their heads: and all may know that those things, whereof they were informed concerning thee, are nothing; but that thou thyself also walkest orderly, and keepest the law. As touching the Gentiles which believe, we have written and concluded that they observe no such thing, save only that they keep themselves from things offered to idols, and from blood, and from strangled, and

116

from fornication. Then Paul took the men, and the next day purifying himself with them entered into the temple, to signify the accomplishment of the days of purification. . . ." The solution they were suggesting to Paul was that he go to the temple with four men who were in the midst of observing the Nazarite vow. Remember this was a vow taken in gratitude for some blessing from God. Those taking the vow practiced abstinence from meat and wine for thirty days and allowed their hair to grow. At the end of this period sacrifices had to be made in the temple and the hair was cut and burned on the altar. It became the practice of wealthy people to take on the responsibility for paying the expenses for those persons who had taken on this vow but were too poor to make the sacrifices. It was this sponsorship that Paul asked to assume so that it could be proven conclusively to the Jews that Paul was not trying to destroy their customs.

Let us not be unaware that this was a difficult thing for Paul to agree to do. It is obvious from other places in the Scriptures that this particular practice was distasteful to Paul. He had written about the superiority of the Christian life over this kind of bondage to ritual and regulation as a means of access to God. But he had also written, "To the Jews I became as a Jew in order to win the Jews, to those under the law I became as one under the law though not myself being under the law that I might win those under the law" (I Cor. 9:20, 21). In this sponsorship Paul evidences his willingness to practice what he had been preaching.

Paul's actions provide for the Christian a guideline for action at those points where one is convinced that some particular matter is insignificant or perhaps even meaningless but must deal with those who are new in the faith or have strong opinions about the importance of that particular act. This is always a live issue for we are always dealing in the church with those who mistake their likes and dislikes for biblical teaching. Recognizing this the Christian will at times be willing to sacrifice his personal opinions for the sake of this weaker brother.

Compromise on matters of opinion is not a sign of weakness but of strength. The sign of a truly great man is his willingness to subordinate his likes and dislikes for the sake of larger issues, namely the harmony of the Church. One of the dearest souls I have ever known is Charles Isaacs, an Elder in the Gardenside Christian Church in Lexington, Kentucky. My respect for him began very early in my ministry. During the course of one of our Board meetings we were having a very decided disagreement on how to carry out a specific task. It was a matter of a method but the various board members had very strong and differing opinions on the particular matter. Charles, after making a very strong defense of his position, was voted down. I waited with some apprehension for his reaction. Would he do as I had seen others do in this situation? Would he blast the board for their un-Christian action. Would he, as some others I've encountered through the years have done, threaten to withhold his tithe if he didn't get what he wanted. Could I expect him to circulate among the congregation rumors of the lack of Christianity either of myself or of the Board? I relaxed and really began to love and respect Charles when he, as recording secretary of the meeting, started to record the vote. He nonchalantly asked, "How do you spell lost?" Here is a man who has learned how to stand strongly for issues that involved personal opinion but when defeated practiced Christian expediency.

The Christian will at times sacrifice some personal habits for his weaker brothers. He will not say, "What I do is my own business." Rather he will say with Paul, "But if thy brother be grieved with thy meat, now walkest thou not charitably. Destroy not him with thy meat, for whom Christ died. Let not then your good be evil spoken of" (Rom. 14:15, 16).

However the Christian must never feel under any obligation to surrender his freedom in Christ even for the sake of harmony. He freely chooses to bow to the opinions of his weaker brother. However he refuses to compromise his own convictions when others make opinions a matter of faith. This Paul refused to do and so should we. Paul could circumsize Timothy even though he knew that Old Testament obligation had been obliterated by the Cross. However in Galations 2:3 he relates his refusal to circumsize Titus because the Judaizers demanded this as a condition for one being accepted as a Christian. This was not a matter of faith and to accept it as such would bring the Christian again into bondage from whence Christ had freed him.

So then the Christian practice of expediency demands that I at times give in on matters of personal opinion. It does not demand that I allow others to impose on me as matters of faith their personal opinion. Our brothers in Christ are free to have opinions on mission methods, millennial theories, musical instruments, the order and type of worship service or a hundred other matters. But we must insist that we also have freedom in these areas and that we not be forced to conform to their opinions.

II. In these Scriptures we see that one manifests a quality commitment by how he reacts to people who are acting

119

out of unwarranted assumptions. Luke records that the Asian Jews saw Paul in the temple and they stirred up people saying, "This is the man that teacheth all men everywhere against the people and the law and this place: and moreover he brought Greeks into the temple and defiled the holy place. For they had before seen him in the city with Trophimus the Ephesian *whom they supposed* Paul had brought into the temple. . . . They laid their hands on Paul and dragged him out of the temple . . . seeking to kill him" (Acts 21:27, 30).

These Jews from Ephesus knew Trophimus. Later when they came on Paul in the Court of Israel they assumed Trophimus was still with him. This was a serious matter. For a Gentile to be in the Court of Israel was a capital offense. The Jews had printed notices in Greek and Latin fixed on the barrier at the foot of the step leading to this inner Court warning the Gentiles not to enter. Two of these notices, one now residing in the Turkish State museum in Istanbul and the other in the Palestinian Museum, state, "No foreigner may enter within the barricade which surrounds the temple and enclosure. Any one doing so will have himself to blame for his ensuing death." The importance of this is seen in that the Romans respected this so much that they ratified this sentence even when it was passed on a Roman citizen. It's interesting to note that in verse 38 of the 21st Chapter, the Roman Tribune also was operating on a mistaken assumption. He said, "Are you not the Egyptian then who recently stirred up the revolt and led the 4,000 men of the Assassins out into the wilderness?" If Paul had been guilty of either of these offenses he could have been legally subject to being executed. However though he was innocent he was almost killed because of an unwarranted assumption.

The Christian is at times faced with those who act out of unwarranted assumptions. It is easy to fall into this trap ourselves. All of us are tempted to assume that things are so without personal investigation of the facts of the case. It is always a temptation to practice this attitude in the matter of inter-personal relations. We assume, without checking the facts, that what has been told us about someone's words or actions is true. Operating on the assumption of the individual's guilt we either pass on the story or that assumption tends to affect our relationship with that person from that day forward. In this too many of us demonstrate the attitude of the man, who as a part of a jury trying a case, walked into the jury room and said immediately, "I vote guilty." The chairman of the jury responded, "how can you do that? We haven't reviewed the facts." Replied the juryman, "I don't have to. I say if he ain't guilty what's he doing here."

Jesus faced this same situation when Pilate asked him in the early hours of his trial, "Are you the King of the Jews?" Jesus replied, "Do you say this of your own accord or did others say it to you about me?" (John 18:34). He was asking Pilate if he had really investigated the facts of the case or if he had been talking to Annas and Caiphas and had been convinced by them that Jesus was a revolutionary and as such a menace to Rome. It is interesting to note that from Pilate's reply he was guilty of the charge (John 18:35).

It is even more of a temptation for persons to operate on unwarranted assumptions in matters of biblical faith. Far too many of us operate on the principle that what is traditional is biblical; that what is being done is what God

121

has commanded to be done. Because we operate on these assumptions we never study the Scriptures to see if these are warranted by facts. A number of illustrations could be cited to substantiate this practice. Such things, for instance, as calling sprinkling baptism. No competent biblical scholar would ever try to defend sprinkling on the basis of the Scripture. Yet sprinkling and pouring are so deeply ingrained in church traditions that to insist on the importance of immersion is to bring on one the accusation that they are bigots who are creating disharmony in the church and destroying the ecumenical spirit.

Extra congregational authorities are traditional rather than biblical. There is no biblical warrant for the ecclesiastical structures that dominate our church scene. Yet many religious people accept them because they assume they are grounded in biblical truth.

The use of denominational names as religious designations are particularly significant in this area of tradition as opposed to Bible. These names came into existence as a result of people swarming around strong personalities who came preaching Christ or as a result of groups emphasizing a neglected aspect of the Christian message. In most instances these Christian leaders were very disturbed that people were elevating the leader instead of holding up the Christ whom they proclaimed. But it did not keep their followers from putting the names of these men or the particular practice being emphasized on the front of their meeting places.

This acting out of an unwarranted assumption is a great temptation as it relates to our Christian service. One of the great dangers in the church is that of utopianism. This is the attitude of those who feel they must be able to do

122

something perfect before they will attempt it at all. Eric Stork, deputy assistant minister of the United States Environmental Automotive Pollution Control could not be considered soft. He has been very hard on businesses that pollute the air. But he makes this significant statement as it relates to the matter of utopianism in social action. "The nation may have bitten off more than it can chew when it has set such high air pollution control goals. Although it is not explicitly stated in the clean air act the law in effect has been interpreted to require that emissions be controlled to the point at which, for example, the worst emphysema victim on the second worst inversion day of the year should be able to spend eight hours at the busiest street corner of the most polluted city without suffering any ill effects from carbon monoxide. When stated in that way our goals tend to be uncomfortable."

This utopianism unfortunately has slipped into the church and into the thinking of sincere believers. I'm not talking about those people who excuse themselves from activity in the Lord's kingdom out of laziness. Nothing less than a conversion experience will ever change their attitude. I am talking about those who refuse to become involved out of a sense of just not being adequate to the task they have been asked to assume. In order to save ourselves from falling to this error we need to remember that this is no ordinary work to which we are called. This a mandate from the Master. When God calls us to the task He will provide the power to carry it to a successful conclusion. If we will exercise our faith God will because of our faith, take our talent and expand it beyond our fondest expectations. This is what the parable of the talents is all about. It is God telling us that abilities used will be stretched and more more effective through exercise.

123

The reaction of the apostle Paul gives us guidelines in confronting these unwarranted assumptions. "I am a Jew of Tarsus of Cilicia, a citizen of no mean city: and I beseech thee, give me leave to speak unto the people" (Acts 21:39). His speech was a refutation of this false assumption. Paul is saying, "The way one handles such unwarranted assumptions is with facts." If the problem is a matter of character assassination the person being slandered has a right to publicly or privately defend himself. If it is a matter of Christian doctrine the answer is an honest and thorough study of the Word of God on these matters. If it is a matter of personal involvement then we need to prayerfully approach God about our responsibility.

III. Luke in this section of Scripture provides a guideline to Christians showing that expresses the quality of their commitment through their willingness and ability to communicate Christ to their world. In Acts 22:1, the apostle begins his testimony by saying, "Brethren and fathers, hear ye the defense that I now make unto you." Having been dragged out of the temple and, but for the intervention of the Roman soldiers garrisoned in the tower of Antonio would have been speedily slain, the apostle now stands before this mob to defend himself. Rather than recant his faith and pleading for his life, Paul recounted his relationship with Jesus Christ. When his faith was tested, the apostle not only held onto the faith that for so many years had held him but he took the opportunity to share that faith with those with whom that faith had come in conflict.

Notice in the words contained in these twenty-one verses that Paul expresses the fundamental methodology of Christian witnessing. First, he identifies himself with the people whom he is trying to reach. "I am a Jew, born in Tarsus of Cilicia, and brought up in this city at the feet of Gamaliel, instructed according to the strict manner of the law of our Fathers, being zealous for God even as you all are this day" (Acts 22:3). He does not talk down but relates to others in their common need. If we are to reach others they must understand that we are all part of the same flesh and blood, that we have the same problems, temptations, needs, hopes, fears, and dreams. Primarily that "all of us have sinned and fallen short of the glory of God." Emerson speaks of the ineffectiveness of anyone who does not identify with the hurts of his world. He tells of coming back disgusted from a church service where, "the preacher talked and acted as if he had never lived."

We are shown in this Scripture that the Christian can effectively witness by relating his condition before Christ came into his life. In Acts 22: verses 4, 5, 19 and 20, Paul paints rather a grim picture of himself before Christ conquered his life. He was a persecutor, a bigotted zealot, and by accessory to the crime, a murderer. The sins of most of us may not be so dramatic but they are just as real. We have committed sins both of commission and omission. We may not have committed murder but we have hated. Jesus said this attitude is just as sinful before God. Moreover like the priest and the Levite we can be condemned not because we have actually injured others but because we have ignored their needs and passed by on the other side. "None of us are righteous, no, not one" (Rom. 3:10).

Through his testimony Paul expresses the validity of Christians telling of their actual conversion experience, Acts 22:6-16 relates for us Paul's testimony as to how he came into the kingdom of God. Paul's conversion began,

125

he said, when he met the Resurrected Lord and through that meeting came to faith in Christ as Lord and Master. This faith led him to a repentant state. In verses 8 and 9 Paul recounts himself as saying, "Who are you, Lord?" and hearing the reply, "I am Jesus whom thou persecutest." In verse 10 Paul reports himself as saying, as an open expression of repentance, "Lord, what will you have me to do?"

Luke reports the final act that brought the apostle into a saving relationship with Jesus Christ as transpiring in Acts 22:16. He reports the apostle's testimony that Ananias, a devout servant of God, came to him saying, "Now why tarriest thou? Arise and be baptized and wash away thy sins calling on the name of the Lord."

Luke in this Scripture records not only Paul's record of his conversion but also of his commission by God. Paul recounts God's words to him in the temple, "And he said unto me: Depart: for I will send thee far hence unto the Gentiles" (Acts 22:21).

Paul, in a sense, is a special case in that he was given the specific task of being the Apostle to the Gentiles. However God calls every Christian to some task in his kingdom. Jerome, an early Christian, writes, "Baptism is the ordination of the laity." By this he meant that the same act that places one into the kingdom of God commissions one to the task of proclaiming to the world the Good News that in God's kingdom dwells love and forgiveness.

Finally, in this Scripture Luke reminds us that there will sometimes be a negative response to one's witness of the Christ. The writer of Acts records the mob as responding to Paul's testimony by saying, "Away with such a fellow from the earth for it is not fit he should live" (Acts 22:22).

126

In the New Testament there were a number of occasions when the testimony of godly men and women fell on unresponsive hearts. We need the encouragement of this verse when our witness brings no fruit. These early Christians were not always successful in bringing others to Christ and neither will we be. In these situations we need the comforting reminder that God does not demand that we always be successful. Jesus did not say, "Well done thou good and successful servant." He did say, "Well done thou good and faithful servant."

The difficulty of making concrete one's commitment in any field of service and thus pointing up the quality of that commitment is expressed in the words of Robert Strausz-Hupe, the newly appointed Ambassador to Sweden who was quite candid on the subject of Sweden. He says, "For many years I have taught international relations. Now I have to practice international relations. It is a difficult business to turn theory into actions."

It is also very difficult for the Christian to make concrete his theoretical commitment, "Lord, what will you have me do?" However, when one is willing to practice the principal of expediency, when one handles in the Spirit of Christ those who are acting on unwarranted assumptions and when one is able to communicate one's Faith with clarity and kindness, that person has gone a long way toward turning theory into practice, thus demonstrating a quality of commitment.

THE HIGH COST OF FAITHFULNESS
Hebrews 10:32—12:29

By W. F. Lown

Christian Faithfulness

Proposition: The high cost of faithfulness implies our need of faith, it is seen in examples of faith of others, and it exhorts us to exercise a vital faith of our own.

Introduction:

    A. I do not know who wrote Hebrews, but I thank God the Holy Spirit used him!

        If Paul didn't write it, I imagine he said (if he read it) "Why didn't I say that?"

        He might have read it, for it was written before he died. (written in early 60's; death late 60's)

    B. Hebrews is a book about "better things"

        1. The better Messenger

        2. The better Apostle

        3. The better Priest

        4. The better Covenant

        5. The better Sacrifice

        6. The better Way

    C. Chapters 10:32—12:29 tell us that Faith is that better way.

        Chapter 11:

            a. Called "The Hymn of Faith"

            b. "Faith" used 26 times: "Faithful": used once.

            c. Examples given because they were FAITH-FUL—full of faith.

I. The high cost of faithfulness includes an awareness of the need for faith.

    A. The early days of faith were hard (32)

    1. Written simply "To The Hebrews"
       a. Their dilemma was evaluating the OLD in the light of the NEW covenant.
       b. The epistle was written to help.
    2. Their early days were often fraught with suffering:
       a. Torture (33)
       b. Plundering of property (34)
  B. Having endured, they are urged not to surrender their gains. (35)
    They are exhorted to endure:

> (Isa. 26:20 quoted) "For a little while, and the coming one shall come and shall not tarry; but my righteous one shall live by faith, and if he shrinks back, my soul has no pleasure in him." (37)
>
> (v. 39) "But we are not of those who shrink back and are destroyed, but of those who have faith and keep their souls."

  C. Application:
    1. The early days are hardest for the Christian.
       a. Paul "At my first defense no man took my part." 2 Tim. 4:16
       b. Taunts after my baptism ("Deacon")
       c. It is easier now.
    2. Persecution might come.
    3. Discouragement does come!
    Will we be of those who shrink because life is hard?
    We may not be condemned to die, but we are commissioned to live!

II. The high cost of faithfulness is illustrated in the examples of the faithful of chapter 11.

A. The well-known:
    1. Abel—offering: "Being dead, yet (v. 4)
    2. Enoch—". . . pleased God" (v. 5)
    3. Noah—God's instrument in providing safety for his people. (v. 7)
    4. Abraham—When God called—he went! (v. 8)
    5. Issac, Jacob, Joseph, Moses. (vs. 20-28)

B. The lesser-known:
    (Read 11:29-35)

C. The Unknown:
    (Read 11:36-40)
    ("OTHERS")

D. Application:
    1. These did not get into "Hall of Faith" by wishful thinking
    2. P. H. Welshimer gained the reputation of faithful preacher by 55 years of disciplined service!
    3. Without this you will never get:
        a. a degree
        b. a satisfaction
        c. a lost soul
        d. a heavenly home!

III. The high cost of faithfulness exhorts Christians to exercise a vital faith of their own.

A. "Let us run . . . the race" (12:1, 2)
    1. With perseverance
    2. Looking to Jesus (pioneer and Perfecter) Chief Captain.

B. Let us "Consider Him" (3-6)
    1. Who endured hostility
    2. Who disciplined Himself
    3. A stinging rebuke—(read 4-6)

C. Let us "lift . . . drooping hands" (12)
   1. Strengthen weak knees (12)
   2. Make straight paths (13)
   3. Strive for peace (14)
   4. Obtain grace (15)
D. Let us ". . . come to Mount Zion . . ." (22)
   1. You are not dealing with: (Altar fires, trumpets, etc. . . .)
   2. You *are* dealing with:
      a. heavenly Jerusalem (22)
      b. Angels (22)
      c. The First Born (23)
E. Let us fear to refuse Jesus. (24)

> V 25 "For if they did not escape when they refused him who warned them on earth, much less shall we escape if we reject him who warns from heaven"

F. Application:
   1. Faithfulness is no accident
   2. It does not say, "What do I want to do for God?"
   3. It says, "Lord, what wouldst thou have me to do?"

CONCLUSION:
   A. "Let us be grateful . . ."
      ". . . for receiving a kingdom that cannot be shaken." (v. 28a)
   B. "Let us offer to God acceptable worship. . ."
      1. ". . . with reverence" (v. 28b)
      2. ". . . and awe" (v. 28b)
   C. "For our God is a consuming fire." (v. 28c)

131

FROM THE TABLE TO THE TOWEL
John 13:1-35; 14:15-23

By Knofel Staton

It was the night on which Jesus was betrayed, and it happened while He was instituting the "Lord's Supper." He looked down, saw something, took off His outer garment, fastened a towel around Himself, took a basin of water, and began to wash the feet of His disciples.

What could He have seen to make Him do such a thing? The answer is simple. He saw dirty feet. There were no interstate highways in those days. The roads were rough and dusty. There were no Mustangs or jets—just foot travel with perhaps an occasional ride on a donkey.

So the travelers arrived with dirty and tired feet. They had a real physical need. Have you ever walked all day at the State Fair? How do your feet feel when you get home? Doesn't it feel great to kick off your shoes? Not only do your feet feel better, but your whole self is relieved. And then, to put your feet into a pan of water—oh, how good that feels! A person's whole attitude can be changed with the washing of feet.

Jesus saw a physical need and moved to meet it. The church, the contemporary body of Christ, can learn a significant lesson from this first-century body of Jesus. We must be sensitive to needs about us and move to meet them regardless of what they are. Jesus does not teach us to meet only the "spiritual" needs of mankind. How much more physical can you get than washing dirty feet! And yet Jesus could do that, because He cared. He cared because He was God in flesh. God cares for the whole man. He created us in our psychosomatic completeness and does not divide us up into parts—a physical part, an emotional

132

part, or a spiritual part. He sees our needs as personal needs, whatever they are. And so should we.

Washing another's feet in the first century was a humiliating task. A good host would provide water for his guests to wash their own feet, but the host himself would not do the washing. We see a good example of that when Abraham told his guests, "Here's some water, wash your own feet" (Gen. 18:4). Laban did the same thing (Gen. 24:32). In fact, it was such a humiliating task that the Jewish law prohibited the householder from making his house slave do it; the slave could legally refuse to do so.

No one ever washed another's feet unless he was considering that person to be better than himself—and then voluntarily took the role of a servant to the other. We see only two examples of it in the Bible—Abigail (I Sam. 25:41) and Jesus. Wives would do so for their husbands, and children would do so for their parents. Isn't it interesting that Jesus began to do what only women and children did —the act of slave-service?

The church must learn that no need of another exists which is below our dignity to touch.

But when Jesus came to wash Peter's feet, Peter rebuked Him, "You are not going to wash my feet!" Peter's arrogance would not let Jesus serve him. And then Jesus said, "If I do not wash you, you have no part in me."

In that statement, Jesus gave us one of His most profound truths about the nature of fellowship. The word "part" is used in the Greek (among other ways) to designate the contribution that an individual makes to the other members of the body of Christ. Christian fellowship can never be restricted to just the Table of our Lord—to the rituals and assemblies. Jesus was saying to Peter, "the kind

133

of fellowship I want with you must include the sharing of needs with one another. You have a need and I want to meet it because I care. If you will not let me meet it, then we cannot really have fellowship with one another."

The church must learn from this. We need to be open to one another's needs and allow other Christians to meet our needs. Christian fellowship is to include the use of the towel (in both the giving and receiving of it) as well as the use of the Table. It is at this level of fellowship that we often fail, for we do not know one another's needs. Too often when we have a need, we are reluctant to share it with another Christian. We keep our "dirty feet" hidden. Our arrogance will not allow us to let another Christian really "see" us.

Instead we take our needs to non-Christians. We would rather borrow money from a pagan loan company than to tell a Christian brother about our need. When we do that we are keeping our fellowship at a distance. We confine our fellowship to once a week around the Table and never get to really know one another. We prevent others from expressing their love. Keeping our needs to ourselves will prevent us from fulfilling the Magnificent Commission which I will consider later.

Peter understood what Jesus meant, so he said, "Not only wash my feet, but all of me." But Jesus replied, "No, I will just wash your feet." Why? Because only Peter's feet *needed* washing. In that reply, Jesus was saying, "Peter, I am not washing feet just to keep busy. I am meeting needs that are *real* needs."

The church today must be busy meeting needs which are *real* needs in the community. We must not just keep busy for activity's sake. It is not impressive to have the lights on in the church building every night just to have a full calendar. We might meet more needs if we closed the building some nights to release the people to meet some needs they see all about them.

Jesus made it clear that His movement from the Table to the towel was to become the marching orders for His people. "I have given you an example, that you also should do as I have done to you." And then He said, "A servant is not greater than His master." If Jesus could take the role of a slave for another person, then we are to do the same. The church's influence rests upon our doing it. For servanthood is the route to Christian leadership. Jesus made that clear when His disciples asked Him who was the greatest in the Kingdom. Jesus replied, "Whoever would be great among you must be your slave" (Matt. 20:27). He made it clear that leadership did not come in the package of dictatorship but in humiliating sacrificial service.

Not only is servanthood the route to Christian leadership, but also to Christian witness. Jesus summed up this thought in what I call "The Magnificent Commission" (John 13:34). "A new commandment I give to you!" There are two ways something can be new—new in time, like a brand new car; or new in usage, like a 1924 Ford that has never been driven. This commandment of Jesus was not *new* in time. In fact, John in I John tells us that it has been around from the beginning. It was *new* in usage—it was still fresh; no one had been busy trying to wear it out. In other words, Jesus was saying, "A fresh, unused commandment I give to you."

And this is the commandment, "that you love one another. . . ." Now if Jesus had stopped there it would not have been so tough to follow, but here comes the tough part,

135

"just the way I have loved you." That's tough, and yet that is what makes the commandment magnificent. This calls me to care for you the way Jesus would if He were here in a 6'2" body. And that calls for you to care for me in that same way.

Jesus continued in verse 35, "By this all men will know that you are my disciples, if you have love for one another." What Jesus didn't say in verse 35 is as important as what He did say. He didn't say, "By this shall all men know you are my disciples if you have the correct name on your church building, or if you never miss the Lord's Supper (isn't *that* interesting since He said this in the midst of the Supper?), or if you always bow your head for prayer in a restaurant, or if you always carry a New Testament." I am not belittling any of those actions, but I'm merely asking that we allow Jesus to mean what He said.

Jesus gave this Magnificent Commission before He gave the Great Commission with good reason. Unless we Christians can love one another, we have just been kidding ourselves if we think we can be very effective witnessing to the world. The world knows that we cannot love them if we do not love each other.

But what does it mean to love one another the way Jesus loved? In English we use only one word to say "love." My little daughter says, "I love Winnie-the-Pooh. I love school. I love Mommy and Daddy." But she has a different kind of love in mind for each one of those. We say, "I love my car and I love my wife." We have a different kind of love in mind, or at least I hope your love for your car is different than your love for your wife! For we get rid of our cars when they get old!

The Greeks had a different word for each different kind of love. They used the word *eros* to mean a selfish love.

A person who does something for another only for what he himself will get out of it is practicing *eros* love. A person who gives to charity primarily for the tax deduction or to get his name put on a building is practicing *eros*. Jesus never commanded us to practice that kind of love.

Another word for love was *philos*. This is a two-way love. It is the love between two friends. It is a give-and-take love. A person with this love will give to another and expect to receive something in return. But Jesus did not command us to practice that kind of love.

Another word that was used for love was *agape*. This is the love that: (1) sees a need and moves to meet it, (2) does not count the cost, (3) does not calculate a return, (4) does not consider the worth of the person with the need, (5) makes decisions for the well-being of the other person. That is the love Jesus commanded us to practice.

Now comes the big question, "How can we love like that?" There are two ways to answer the "how." One way is how-practically; that is, *what* can we do. The other way is how-preparationally; that is, how can we be *equipped*. Let us look at these ways.

To love practically we must first of all see needs. That means we must become more sensitive to the people about us. But what are some of the needs of Christians? Christians have both general and specific needs. We all have the general needs; our specific needs vary with each individual.

Let us consider some of our general needs. Growing Christians have some of the same kind of needs that growing children have. It is not just verbiage that new Christians are called new-born babes. Guess what has been discovered is the first basic need of a new-born babe? It is the need to be touched, talked to, and caressed—in short, the need for affection and fellowship. A baby who doesn't have that need met will be more susceptible to physical diseases and emotional sickness the rest of his life.

But often that is what a new-born babe doesn't get. As soon as he is born, he is often taken a half block away from the mother to a nursery. Now many hospitals are seeing the fallacy of this and changing their practices.

Just as a new-born babe, the new Christian needs dynamic *personal* fellowship. But often he doesn't get it. Interpersonal alienation often begins just before his delivery, especially if the church service has gone over-time and he wants to be baptized now. We think, "Oh, why couldn't he wait until tonight?" Then after the baptism, he comes into the sanctuary to find—no one there. Many have told me how depressing an experience that was for them.

The new Christian needs to be with a new brother or sister during the coming week, but often that never happens. It isn't long before a new-born baby needs nourishment— the milk kind. And the new Christian needs the *milk* of the Word. But how many new Christians have been choked with the meaty words like "sanctification," "propitiation," "expiation," or "justification?" Why is it that we give the new Christian the same diet as those who have been Christians for forty years?

Soon we encourage the new-born baby to walk. I'll never forget when our children took their first steps. We worked with them several weeks, and then finally they took two or three steps on their own. Then what? Each one fell flat on his face! But I did not get upset and yell or say they were no good. I picked them up and said, "that's a fine job." What is good about falling? They would never have

138

fallen if they had not tried. If I had belittled them when they fell, they might have become discouraged from trying again.

When a new Christian falls spiritually, we must do for him what we would do for a child—pick him up and help him —not step on him! That is what Paul said in Galatians 6, "when a brother is overtaken in a fault, you who are spiritual restore him in the spirit of gentleness and meekness."

Falling is not reserved for the young. A couple of years ago, my wife and I were leaving a meeting; it was late at night. Our children were asleep; my wife carried our son, while I carried our daughter. My wife, Julia, got off balance and fell flat. I did not yell at her, "What is the matter with you? Don't you know how to walk? I knew that what your mother taught you would never last; she used too much emotion!" No, I helped her up and helped her to the car. And in the car I said, "From now on when the kids fall asleep, I will always carry the heavier one. That is probably why you got off balance."

When a Christian brother falls spiritually, we should ask ourselves, "I wonder what burden he is carrying that I could help him carry?" Paul also said in Galatians 6:2, "Bear one another's burdens and so fulfill the law of Christ."

It is not long before babies learn to talk. They learn to talk from hearing others talk. And so it is with Christians. We not only need each other to walk the talk but also to talk the walk. Have you noticed how young Christians want to talk about the Lord? If we stifle that by only talking about the weather or politics, then they will soon be talking about only the weather and politics.

There are many other needs, but I want to consider just one more—the need to edify our brothers and sisters by the way we speak to them and about them. It has been discovered that the way we speak to and about people actually affects their physical health. "There is one whose rash words are like sword thrusts, but the tongue of the wise brings healing" (Prov. 12:18).

But how can we possibly love like this? What can equip us to love the way Jesus loved? The only way we can love the way Jesus loved is to have Jesus living within us. In John 14 He promises His disciples that He Himself will live in them through the Holy Spirit.

God pours His kind of love (*agape*-style) into our hearts through the Holy Spirit. "For the fruit of the Spirit is love . . ." (Gal. 5:27). God's love can live in you as you turn from your selfishness to God's Savior, as you decide to quit living as a master and begin living as a servant, and as you open your life to the equipment of the greatest servant who ever lived—Jesus. Peter put it this way, "Repent and be baptized every one of you in the name of Jesus Christ for the forgiveness of your sins; and you shall receive the gift of the Holy Spirit" (Acts 2:38).

That Holy Spirit is the presence of Jesus Himself. So Jesus not only expects us to live out His Magnificent Commission, but He also equips us to do it. And He became our example by moving from the Table to the Towel and later from Gethsemane to Calvary. With Calvary clearly in front of Him, He said, "A new commandment I give to you, that you love one another; even as I have loved you, that you also love one another. By this all men will know that you are my disciples, if you have love for one another." And also (John 14:18, 20), "I will not leave you desolate; I will come to you. In that day you will know that I am in my Father, and you in me, and I in you."

140

MAN'S GREATEST NEED: FORGIVENESS
Psalm 51

By Charles R. Gresham

Introduction:

Nathan, the prophet, walked boldly into the throne room of Israel. David, the King, beckoned him forward. Nathan began a story: "There were two men in a certain city, the one rich, the other poor. The rich man had great flocks and herds; the poor man had nothing but one little ewe lamb. He cherished it, nourished it; his children played with it; it was like a household pet, eating from his hand, drinking from his cup, sleeping on his bed, yes . . . more, a member of the family."

"Meanwhile a traveler stopped at the rich man's home. Unwilling to take from his own vast flocks, to prepare a feast for the guest; he took the poor man's ewe lamb, slaughtered it and prepared it for his guest."

David's anger grew as the story unfolded. He exploded: "The man who did this deserves to die and he shall make restitution fourfold. That was a dastardly, pitiless deed."

Nathan's bony finger slowly lifted and was pointed straight at the King, and quietly he said in the hush that followed the King's outburst: "You are that man!" Immediately, David's recent sins came flooding before him. You have killed Uriah! Murderer! You have taken his wife! Adulterer! You have sinned!

Under the prodding of the prophet's words; David's guilty conscience was stricken and he cried out "I have sinned against the Lord." Nathan replied: "You shall not die; the Lord has put away your sin" (2 Samuel 12:1-15).

This is the background of Psalm 51 which is "the classic in the literature of penitence. No poem or prayer equals it in depth of feeling or ardour of utterance. It has proved itself both a challenge and a solace to innumerable men and women who in a lightning flash of self-revelation have been filled with self-loathing and longing for reconciliation with God" (*Speakers Bible* "Psalm 51").

Here in this Psalm growing out of the reality of human experience, man's greatest need is highlighted—*Forgiveness, Reconciliation with God.* So in all ages of man's hymnody, man's true condition recognized as sinful—out of harmony with God—has caused him to cry out for forgiveness.

The tragedy of our modern age is expressed in the title (and the content) of a recent book, *Whatever Became of Sin?* Written not by a preacher, or theologian or moralist but by the most outstanding psychiatrist of the 20th Century— Karl Menninger of the famed Menninger Clinic of Topeka, Kansas. From his experience he points out how in our modern society we tend not only to *minimize sin,* but, often, clearly, deny it. As a result, sin's real nature as responsible evil is either ignored or just not recognized. The results however continue unabated in human misery, broken and frustrated lives and ungodly rebellion. Such tragedy merely highlights the truth expressed in this great Psalm —Man's greatest problem is *sin* and man's greatest need is *forgiveness.*

Note the development in this Penitential Poem.

I. A Cry for Mercy (verses 1, 2)

The appeal is to God's mercy, God's lovingkindness. This is the only approach the honest man can make. He cannot deny his sin; he cannot shift blame and responsibility onto someone else or some circumstance. Like David, he stands naked before the piercing eye of God's prophet and the bony finger of judgment and cries, "Have mercy on me, O God."

142

The cry for mercy can come only when conscience has revealed that we, indeed, are sinners. And this is the problem with our age; we have so lulled our consciences; so excused ourselves; so redefined sin; that we can no longer recognize what sin really is. But, when those times come—as they did to David, so they will come to us—like evil Richard III we too will confess:

> O coward conscience, how thou dost aflict me!
> The light burns blue. It is now dead midnight.
> Cold, fearful drops stand on my trembling flesh.
>
> My conscience hath a thousand several tongues,
> And every tongue brings in a several tale,
> And every tale condemns me.
>
> All several sins . . .
> Throng to the bar crying all Guilty! Guilty!
> (*King Richard III, Act V, Sec. 3*)

This is a terrifying, shattering experience; but it is necessary if we are to seek the only help possible for a troubled conscience and sin-blasted life. "Have mercy on me, O God."

The appeal is to God's mercy and lovingkindness but the remedy is immediately seen—"blot out my transgressions." "Wash me thoroughly from my iniquities." "Cleanse me from my sin." Note the address is to God who alone can supply the remedy requested. But *note also* the personal pronouns *my* sin, *my* transgressions, *my* iniquities. Here is the starting point—a dual recognition of my sinfulness and God's mercy and graciousness.

II. A Confession of Sin (verses 3-6)

Sin cannot be forgiven and the sinner cleansed until confession is made. Confession means recognition. The Psalmist emphasizes that he is aware of his sin. "For I know my transgressions, and my aim is ever before me."

But more, his sin is against God! "Against thee and thee only have I sinned." He has spoiled his fellowship with God! It is so easy to dismiss sin as but human failure, mistake and error if sin has only horizontal consequences— that is, if it affects only others. So David could have argued, relative to Uriah's death and his adultery: "Bathsheba is better off and Uriah would have died in some other battle."

This is why the heartless Lady MacBeth walks in her sleep, rubbing her hands, trying to wash the invisible blood away muttering, "Out, out, damned spot." She had sinned! Not against Duncan, but the God of Heaven.

This is why in the Scarlet Letter of Hawthorne Arthur Dimmesdale, though living a life of purity and giving himself to others as a Christian Minister, could never find peace until he took his stand beside that silent one with whom he had secretly sinned. He had sinned against God.

"I have sinned against Heaven and in thy sight" is the confession wrung from the heart of the prodigal when he came to Himself and went home.

It is this perspective on sin that reaches to such cosmic heights—"Against thee and thee only"—that causes the Psalmist to confess his utter despair in the human situation. His sin, sin against God as well as man, led him to acknowledge a universal taint and disgrace. Ah "twas in sin that my mother conceived me, in iniquity was I brought forth." The last trace of self-complacency is shattered. Unclothed, unarmoured, unweaponed, he lies before God. He has neither resources, nor merits, nor offerings to present. He knows himself without excuse, and without resource" (The Speakers Bible, Ps. 51).

The depth of his confession is apparent in his desire to open his inner-most heart, his very core of being to God's forgiveness and truth and to ask God "to teach wisdom in his secret heart." Confession leads not to just a new start; but a new nature in the recesses of one's inner-most being.

III. A Plea for Cleansing (verses 7-12)

Awareness, Confession, Cleansing. This is the proper order! The Psalmist pleads for cleansing. Here is no "modern feeling," as Dean Inge notes, which goes back "to the pre-Christian way of looking at evil as an imperfection to be set right, rather than a dark stain to be washed out in tears and blood."

"Purge me with hyssop and I shall be clean, wash me and I shall be whiter than snow" cries the Psalmist, reflecting Isaiah 1:18. "Come, let us reason together saith the Lord, though your sins be as scarlet, they shall be as wool; though they be red like crimson, they shall be as snow." "Hide thy face from my sin." This is reflected by that bit of verse written by some unknown poet:

My Sins Are Gone

I will cast all thy sins in the depth of the Sea,
All thy sins and transgressions, whatever they be:
Though they mount up to Heaven though they go down
    to Hell,
I have buried them there, and above them shall swell,
All my waves of forgiveness so boundless and free.
I have cast all thy sins in the depth of the Sea.

—Unknown

But cleansing is not only outward, it is inward. The Psalmist pleads: "Fill me with joy and gladness" (verse 8); "Create in me a clean heart" (verse 10); "Restore to me the joy of my salvation" (verse 12); "and uphold me with a willing spirit." (verse 12).

And such cleansing makes room for the Holy Spirit. "Take not thy Holy Spirit from me" (verse 11). As J. Edwin Orr phrases it:

> Search me, O Lord, and know my heart, I pray
> Try me, O master, and know my thoughts today
> See if there be some wicked way in me
> Cleanse me from every sin and set me free.

IV. A Vow of Consecration (verses 13-17)

"Then". . . how significant this small particle! When I acknowledge my sin, confess it as against God as well as my fellow, and find cleansing and forgiveness THEN, and only then, can I truly make a vow of consecrated life. The Psalmist vows:

> "I will teach transgressors thy ways";
> "I will help sinners return to Thee";
> "My tongue will sing aloud of Thy forgiveness";
> "My lips will be open and my mouth filled with praise"
> (verses 13-15).

Why? Because "God has delivered me from blood guiltiness"—the God of my salvation (verse 14) and He has shown me that He desires "a broken and contrite heart" (verses 16-17).

We are saved to serve; forgiven to forgive; pardoned to praise; and we sing with joy that little chorus:

> Gone, gone, gone, gone, Yes my sins are gone;
> Now my soul is free and in my heart's a song.
> Buried in the deepest Sea, Yes that's good enough for me,
> And I shall live eternally, Praise God, my sins are gone.

Man's greatest need is forgiveness. But God promises forgiveness on the basis of his own atoning grace through Jesus Christ. John Bunyan in *Pilgrim's Progress,* in his dream, sees Pilgrim going up a highway fenced by a wall on either side; that wall was called *Salvation.* Burdened by the heavy load of Sin on his back he made his way with difficulty. He ran until he came to a place somewhat ascending and upon that place stood a Cross and, a little below in the bottom, a sepulchre. Just as Christian came up to the Cross, his burden was lifted from his shoulders and fell from his back and began to tumble, and so continued till it came to the mouth of the open tomb, where it fell in and was seen no more.

But Forgiveness is demanding! It demands that we forgive others; but, more difficult sometimes, it demands that we forgive ourselves. Wordsworth, in *The Excursion* tells of the minister who speaks of a person unable to forgive himself, who consequently took his own life:

> Much to the last remained unknown: but this
> Is sure, that through remorse and grief he died;
> Though pitied among men, absolved by God,
> He could not find forgiveness in himself;
> Nor could endure the weight of his own shame
> *(Bk. VI).*

To accept Forgiveness is to accept what God offers; to fail to do so is to insult the living God whom we have insulted for too long by our sin.

But to accept forgiveness means to accept all those responsibilities consequent upon the new life; it means to seek continuous forgiveness.

"If any one sin, we have an advocate" (I John 2:1) writes John in this his first epistle, but he also says, "I am writing that you sin not." So as John Oxenham says to the one newly cleansed:

> Bolt that door!
> Each sin has its door of entrance.
> Keep-that-door-closed!
> Bolt it tight!
> Just outside the wild beast
> Crouches in the night.
> Pin the bolt with a prayer,
> God will fix it there.

FOUR PLANKS IN THE PLATFORM OF NEW TESTAMENT CHRISTIANITY

(Genesis 26:17-19)

By Marshall Leggett

Some time ago I had occasion to speak on the same platform with Dr. Carl Ketcherside. Dr. Ketcherside is a most incisive thinker and precise speaker. He said, "Brethren, we have nothing of which to be ashamed, we have something to share." A number of years ago now, the Episcopal rector who ministered across the street from First Christian Church, Canton, Ohio, crossed Cleveland Avenue and visited the evening services of that congregation. At the invitation hymn he stepped forward and was baptized. Following the baptism he said to Brother P. H. Welshimer, "Sir, you people have the greatest plea on earth but you are the stingiest with it."

This is much the way I feel about the movement to restore the essence of New Testament Christianity to its pristine purity. I feel that we do not have so much of which to be ashamed, as we have something to share. We probably have the greatest plea on earth but we are the stingiest with it.

So, if you have ever wondered why the congregations of the Restoration movement are called, "Christian Churches" and "Churches of Christ"? If you have ever wondered why the members of those churches are called simply "Christians" only? If you have ever wondered why our churches are autonomous, interdependent congregations under the leadership of the elders with the help of the deacons? If you have ever wondered why we practice Christian baptism as the immersion of a believer for the remission of sins that he may receive the gift of the Holy Spirit? If you have ever wondered why the Lord's Supper is served every Lord's Day in our worship? If you have ever wondered why the Bible is so respected and reverenced in our midst? If you

149

have ever wondered about any of these questions, you can be sure that this message has been prepared with you in mind.

This evening I should like to offer you "four planks" in the platform of New Testament Christianity. These planks are four early leaders of the movement and what they stood for. They are: Barton Warren Stone and The The Ancient Name; Thomas Campbell and The Ancient Book; Alexander Campbell and The Ancient Order of Things; and Walter Scott and The Ancient Gospel. These early leaders, like their predecessor in faith, Isaac, redug some old wells of their fathers and they too found wells of springing water.

I. Barton Warren Stone and the Ancient Name

Back at the turn of the nineteenth century settlers poured across the Appalachian Mountains much more rapidly than the church could keep up with them. This caused a spiritual vacuum on the American frontier. It was the age of the old circuit rider when a preacher would ride into a community, perhaps only once every four or five months, and preach. The census of 1800 showed that fewer than 10 percent of the settlers west of the Appalachian Mountains had any active relationship with a church at that time.

We have an old rule in church history which says, "God cannot stand a vacuum." He cannot stand a vacuum in the natural realm. This is the reason for the thunder. The lightning streaks through the sky crowding out the air pressure. The roll and rumble of the thunder is merely the pressure rushing back into the vacuum because God's nature will not tolerate a vacuum. It is the reason that when you throw a light bulb against the wall it pops. The light bulb is a vacuum protected by glass. When the shield is broken, the air pressure rushes in to fill the void. God cannot stand a vacuum in the natural realm and He can't stand one in the spiritual realm either.

Rushing in to fill the spiritual vacuum on the American frontier was what is called the old camp meeting. It was when people would ride their horses or travel in wagons sometimes hundreds of miles, camp out, and spend days listening to preaching. The largest of these camp meetings on the American frontier was held north of Lexington, Kentucky, in Bourbon County, at a place called Cane Ridge. Historians say that 25,000 people gathered for this meeting. If this figure is true, it represents one out of every twenty persons west of the Appalachian Mountains at that time. The meeting was very emotional. They say that they swooned, they stayed in trances for hours, and some "yapped" like dogs. One feature of the Cane Ridge meeting was its interdenominational nature. A Baptist would preach from a rock, a Methodist would preach from a stump, and a Presbyterian would preach from the back of a wagon. But, seemingly to the people involved, the Holy Spirit blessed each man's preaching equally.

Participating in this Cane Ridge Revival was a Presbyterian preacher whose name was Barton Warren Stone. Stone was much impressed by what had gone on in the great camp meeting. When he returned to his pastoral duties at Cane Ridge Presbyterian Church, he sat down and began to think. He said to himself, "I can find nowhere that God ever commanded me to be a Presbyterian. All He has ever said He wanted me to be is a Christian only." This led Stone to write a very important document. It is entitled, "The Last Will and Testament of the Springfield Presbytery." The document tells of the Cane Ridge Church leaving the denomination to become simply a Christian Church composed of those who would be Christians only.

Barton Warren Stone "dug an old well" of his forefathers and gave us the ancient name "Christians." It is a most meaningful and beautiful name. It is both inclusive and exclusive. It includes all of those who love Christ and seek to follow in His way. Every person in every denomination is proud to be called a "Christian." However, it excludes all of those who will not accept Christ as their Lord. For the name literally means "to belong to Christ." Barton Warren Stone gave us the ancient name "Christian."

II. Thomas Campbell and The Ancient Book

At about the same time, there was ministering in Western Pennsylvania near Washington, an Anti-burgher, New Light Seceder Presbyterian by the name of Thomas Campbell. Campbell had immigrated to this country from Scotland. Ministering on the western frontier, he became convinced that the denominational structure of Christendom was not merely unfortunate but was basically evil. It not only divided God's people but it was confusing to the unbelievers. As providence would have it, a group of independent Presbyterians visited a Presbyterian congregation to which he was ministering. As providence would have it, it was communion Sunday. Campbell ordered his men to serve the independent Presbyterians the emblems of communion. This was against the rules of the Presbyterian denomination. The synod promptly censured Campbell. One story says that his punishment was that he was to preach a sermon to the pigs. The sermon was to be a full length dissertation, taken to the sty, and preached to its inhabitants. This story sounds more like legend than truth. However, Campbell bitterly resented the censure.

So, he too sat down and wrote a famous document. It was entitled, "The Declaration and Address." It begins something like this, "The Church of Jesus Christ upon earth is essentially, intentionally, and constitutionally one; consisting of all those in every place that profess their faith in Christ and obedience to Him in all things according to the Scriptures." Campbell came to the conclusion that if people would follow the Bible only they would become Christians only. He eschewed denominational creeds and confessions of faith. He felt they were man made and devisive.

It was Thomas Campbell who redug the old well of his forefathers and gave us the ancient Book, the Bible. Campbell was committed to the Book. His biography is thus entitled, *Thomas Campbell: Man of the Book*. He felt the Bible was the only rule of faith and practice for the church. He felt that where the Bible spoke, Christian people ought to speak and where the Bible was silent Christian people ought to be silent. He believed that in matters of faith, there should be unity; in matters of opinion, there should be liberty; and in all things, there should be love. Because of this last reason, he began the "Declaration and Address" by addressing it to "all those who love Christ in Sincerity." Thomas Campbell gave us the ancient Book, the Bible.

III. Alexander Campbell and The Ancient Order of Things

Thomas Campbell had a brilliant son by the name of Alexander. He had been left in Scotland with the family to pursue his education. When the family arrived in America, Thomas Campbell rushed to the port of New York to greet them. Eagerly he showed his document, "The Declaration of Address," to his son. Much to his surprise and delight, Alexander informed him that he had come to the same conclusion as his father while studying in Scotland. He too believed that people could become Christians only by following the Bible only.

Alexander was the possessor of a keen intellect. He was particularly gifted in linquistics. He translated the New Testament from its original language in a version called, *The Living Oracles*. Alexander said that, if we were going to be Christians only by following the Bible only, we would have to go precisely by what the Bible taught. So, he took his keenly analytical mind to the task of studying the Scriptures in depth. He said that we must restore the "ancient order of things."

He concluded, for example that the Bible is divided into three parts, not just two. There is, "the starlight age," "the moonlight age," and "the sunlight age." The starlight age was the Patriarchal. The moonlight age was the Mosaical era. And, of course, the sunlight age is the Christian era. Campbell came to the conclusion that the New Testament church was composed of autonomus, interdependent congregations under the leadership of the elders with the help of the deacons. He concluded that Christian baptism was the immersion of the believer for the remission of sins that he might receive the gift of the Holy Spirit. Consequently, he himself was immersed, his family, and even his father, Thomas. He arrived at the conviction that the Lord's Supper was the center of New Testament worship. He felt that the early church, having few preachers and no seminaries, would meet on the Lord's Day around the emblems of the Lord's Supper to remind them of the central fact of the Gospel message that Christ died for their sins.

It was Alexander Campbell who said that if the people were to be Christians only by following the Bible only they must restore the ancient order of things. He said that we must do Bible things in Bible ways and call Bible things by Bible names. He redug an old well by going back to the fountainhead and gave us "the ancient order of things." It has been like a "well of springing water."

IV. Walter Scott and The Ancient Gospel

At about the same time on the Western Reserve, there was an evangelist by the name of Walter Scott. He was much impressed by the teaching of the Campbells. But he said that if we were to be Christians only by following the Bible only and restoring the ancient order of things, we must be able to explain the plan of salvation so simply and rationally that even the little children could understand.

So, he would ride his hourse into a community, gather his children around him, and would say to them, "Little children, do you know what you have to do to become Christians?" Of course, the children did not. They had been reared in Calvinism. Scott would hold up his hand and perform what has become known as "The Five Finger Exercise." There are variations of this. But basically this is what he would say, "Little children, hold up your hand like this. Your thumb represents faith in Christ, the forefinger represents repentance of sins, the middle finger is baptism into Christ, the ring finger represents remission of sins, and the little finger represents the gift of the Holy Spirit." Then he would say, "Little children, go tell your parents what they have to do to become Christians and tell them that a preacher is going to speak on that subject in the schoolhouse this evening."

Whole congregations would leave their denominations to become Christians only as they were moved by this simple, rational explanation of the plan of salvation.

Walter Scott said that to be Christians only by following the Bible only and restoring the ancient order of things, we must be able to explain the plan of salvation so simply that even the little children could understand it. He gave us the ancient Gospel.

These are the "Four Planks in the Platform of New Testament Christianity." They are four early leaders of the movement and what they stood for. Barton Warren Stone and the ancient name, "Christian"; Thomas Campbell and the ancient book, the Bible; Alexander Campbell and the ancient order of things—doing Bible things in Bible ways; and Walter Scott and the ancient Gospel. These were men who like Isaac before them redug old wells that their fathers had used and found wells of springing water that have been passed down even to our generation.

However, the movement to restore the essence of New Testament Christianity to its pristine purity, like any other movement, is only one generation away from extinction. Just fifty years ago historians were saying that the Restoration movement was destined to be lost in "the backwash of church history." It had been inundated by theological modernism. Modernism called into question the inspiration and authoritative nature of Scripture. Many observers felt that this blow struck the "glass jaw" of the movement because the ideal to restore New Testament Christianity was founded firmly on belief that the Bible was God's inspired and authoritative revelation of himself and His will to man. Many of the great institutions of the Restoration movement were swept away by theological modernism and quickly became secularized. It seemed to some that only a remnant of the movement was left. Brother Burris Butler tells me that in 1924 there were only two missionary families abroad who could be counted upon to preach New Testament Christianity. There were only three struggling Bible Colleges on the outer perimeter of the movement who could be depended upon to prepare a minister to preach the ideals of the movement. However, the remnant that was left never lost faith in the "old wells" they had received from their forefathers. With this unyielding faith, they found three tools that, in my opinion, gave rebirth to the Restoration movement for our generation. First, they founded Christian Service Camps for the inspiration of youth. My own ministry is the product of the Christian Service Camp. I spoke at a Bible College some years ago. I asked all the young men who received their inspiration to become preachers in Christian Service Camp to stand. It seemed to me that fully three fourths of all the young men present arose. Then, they started Bible Colleges for the preparation of a ministry. From three small struggling colleges in 1924 the number has grown to be over thirty-five. And some of these are not small when you consider that every person there is considering vocational Christian service. The Methodist preacher in the little community where I formerly ministered used to marvel at the great number of young preachers the Christian Churches had to begin new congregations, revive the dead ones, and to man existing ones. These young preachers were the product of the recruitment and training of the movement's colleges. Finally, the remnant found a publishing company that would publish true to the Bible literature. With their deep convictions and these three tools, the Restoration movement has experienced a phenomenal rebirth. But it seems to me that there is danger of the movement being lost in our generation if it does not redig those same "old wells" that gave living water to our forefathers.

There are three great dangers to the Restoration movement in this generation. The first one I call "pragmatism." Pragmatism is doing what works at the expense of truth. Some of our churches in this age have wanted to grow so much that they have forgotten why they want to grow. The most dangerous form of pragmatism, in my opinion, is emulating Independent Baptist methodology until we inadvertently absorb Baptist theology. I always feel a little guilty when I say this. There is much within the independent Baptists that is admirable. Their evangelistic zeal, their concept of separation from the world, and their demonstration that the "old time religion" (American style) does not work in the twentieth century. However, we must realize that the Independent Baptist is the most Baptist of the Baptist.

One of its famous churches is located in Cincinnati, Ohio. It has a most significant name. Back in the middle part of the nineteenth century there was a movement in Western Kentucky and Tennessee to "re-Baptistize" the Baptist church. It was a conservative movement. It taught that only those baptized by Baptist preachers were scripturally baptized, that only Baptists could take communion in Baptist churches, that only Baptist ministers were ordained of God to marry, and that the Baptist church is the New Testament Church. It traced Baptist history by a circuitous route through the Albigenses back to John the Baptist to try to establish its New Testament Roots. It would be difficult to find a Southern Baptist church historian in this age that would agree with that route. The expressed motive of this effort was to make the Baptist Church more Baptist. The movement was called, "The Landmark Movement," after which the famous church in Cincinnati is named.

We can respect much that has been accomplished by the Independent Baptist but let us always realize that the Independent Baptist is the most Baptist of the Baptists. He is Baptist in his nomenclature, not New Testament. He is Baptist in his doctrine, not New Testament. He is Baptist in his church policy, not New Testament.

Pragmatism can be a danger to the ideal to restore the essence of New Testament Christianity. We must never be guilty of doing what works at the expense of truth.

The second danger to the movement is what is called "neo-pentecostalism." And let me hasten to say that this is a misnomer. The modern phenomenon labeled "neo-pentecostalism" in no way parallels what happened on the Day of Pentecost when the disciples spoke in "other tongues" and men from sixteen different nations each heard in his own native language. It at best could be called, "neo-corinthianism," but I have some doubts about that.

Our forefathers had something to say about the Holy Spirit. In those early days the issue was Calvinism and Arminianism. Both taught the direct, personal intervention of the Holy Spirit in conversion. Alexander Campbell repudiated this. He emphasized the Holy Spirit working through the Word. He said, "It is an overwhelming fact that God does nothing in creation or redemption without His Word."

His position concerning the work of the Holy Spirit was this. He said the Holy Spirit works through the Word. He gave the apostles that which they should preach, the power to do miracles to attest the validity of their message, and preserved it in the Scripture for those who would believe. "God now speaks to us only by His Word," he said. "By

159

His Son, in the New Testament, he has fully revealed Himself and His will. This is the only revelation of the Spirit which we are to regard."

Dr. V. Raymond Edman, former president of Wheaton College, makes a pertinent observation concerning "Neo-Corinthianism." He says, "Glossolalia today is either of the devil, or is a genuine gift of the Spirit, or it is a phenomenon that has been psychologically produced." He went on to say that he prayed that it was not the first alternative. He could not accept the second. He prayed that it was the third. Dr. George D. Cutter, a recognized authority on tongues speaking says, "As far as I know there is no case of speaking in strange tongues which has been strictly and scientifically investigated that cannot be explained by recognized psychological laws." He agrees with Dr. Edman. So do I.

The modern day charismatic movement has failed to divide that which is temporary from that which is both universal and abiding. This misinterpretation can do great harm to the movement to restore the essence of New Testament Christianity.

Another danger I see to the movement in our age is what I call "LETHARGIC LAODICEANISM." And I am sure that when I say that, I have just coined a new phrase. But it represents a lack of dedication, determination, discipline, and zeal on the part of the people of this movement. It is the danger of becoming a cozy little communion and failing to let the message of New Testament Christianity be known. It is the kind of Laodiceanism which made Christ sick in the Book of Revelation.

It seems to me that those dedicated to restoring the essence of New Testament Christianity to its pristine purity

160

have not so much of which to be ashamed as they have something to share. We probably have the greatest plea on earth, but are the stingiest with it. I feel about the Restoration movement the way the five marines advancing up Mt. Surabaja on Iwo Jima in World War II felt about their country. The marines were carrying the American flag to be planted on top of the mountain. They were moving so rapidly that they separated themselves from the main body of troops. The commanding officer called up to them saying, "Slow down. You are moving too rapidly." The answer came back from the marines, "We will not slow down. We will continue to move forward. You bring the troops up to the standard." This seems to be a simple plea of the Restoration ideal. It is to say to the religious world, "Let's bring the troops up to the standard of New Testament Christianity."

Our forefathers dug wells in which they found springs of living water. If we have the wisdom of Isaac, we too will dig those same wells of our forefathers and will find that life-giving spring.

PREACH THE WORD

II Timothy 4:1-5

By Don DeWelt

Introduction: (What is "the word" we preach?)

A king was compelled to go to a prison to find out about our subject. I refer to King Zedekiah and to the prophet Jeremiah. Zedekiah had thrown Jeremiah in prison for preaching the word. Now the king repents. He has no better answer than the word of the Lord which he heard from the lips of God's prophet. "Is there any word from the Lord?" he asks, (Jeremiah 37:16, 17).

What did King Zedekiah mean? He wanted to know if God has programmed the prophet's mind. "Has God spoken to you so you can speak to me?" "The word" he wanted was intuitive information direct from God through the mind and mouth of the prophet Jeremiah. God's spokesman had a word from God, but the king would not like it. He and his nation were to be captured and carried away to Babylon. This was "the word" from the Lord.

If you want to know the word as Jeremiah preached it, you can read it in his book—the second largest book in the whole Old Testament.

Preaching is a public act. "The word" preached was direct revelation from God, either intuitive or written. Today, God has furnished us with His revelation in permanent written form, which is altogether sufficient to furnish us unto every good work, (II Timothy 3:16, 17).

Preaching the word today is preaching the truth as found in the sixty-six books of the Bible. We are *"charged"*— *"commanded"* to preach the Word. If we preach more than what is in the 66 books, it is foolish, and God will add His plagues to us. If we preach less than what we find in the 66 books, He will remove our name from the roll

162

of heaven. We are to preach *only* and always what is contained in the Bible, which is the Word of God.

Proposition: We want to ask and answer five questions from our text about preaching the word.

I. *Who is in our audience as we preach the word?*

"I charge thee in the sight of God, and of Christ Jesus, who shall judge the living and the dead, and by His appearing and His kingdom: (II Tim. 4:1).

A. God, the author.

Every sermon is a "command appearance" before the King of ten million galaxies! How carefully Paul chose his words when he stood before King Agrippa, but it was only because he was conscious of always speaking in the presence of the Almighty God. If the people to whom you address yourself look and act and talk in a very ordinary manner, please do not forget that God appeared to Moses in an ordinary bush in the desert land of Midian.

B. *Before Christ Jesus*—He is there in the Person of the other Comforter. Be careful, be prepared, be encouraged. One day our Lord will come and ask you for an account of this all-important stewardship. The judge of all the living and all the dead is present in your audience. He hears and believes every word you preach from Himself and His Father and His apostles and His prophets. He believes it, and appreciates it, and is pleased with it every time you preach.

Who is the preacher in the little Baptist church in Plains, Georgia? Do you suppose he feels any different when Jimmy is there as when Jimmy is not there? He shouldn't. Jesus our Lord hears everyone every time; the important question is not does it meet with the approval of Jimmy Carter, but of Christ Jesus. The word "appearing" is an interesting one; it means "presence." Pick out one of the vacant spaces and put our Lord in that seat, because He is there!

C. In our audience are the citizens of the Kingdom of our Lord. Be careful; you are talking to *His* subjects, *His* citizens. If you hurt them, you will answer to their King, for they hold the rights of the Eternal Kingdom. They can at any time they want to "appeal to the Supreme Lord" and you will appear with them before Him.

There will be *no* subjects in the Eternal Kingdom that are not *now* citizens of His Kingdom on earth; His body, His church. Inasmuch as you feed His sheep (educate His subjects) you feed Him. Be glad—the same persons to whom you address yourself today will spend all eternity in the eternal Kingdom. Those persons to whom you speak are a royal priesthood, a holy nation, an eternal kingdom!

What an audience—much larger than the North American Christian Convention. I, like Paul, charge you to preach His Word—all of His Word, all the time, only His Word, knowing that it is God, Christ Jesus and His holy citizens who hear you.

In addition to those mentioned in our text are the innumerable host of angels who would love to do what our Lord gave you to do.

164

II. *How and When is the best time to preach?*

". . . preach the word; be urgent in season, out of season," (II Tim. 4:2a).

A. *Urgently "in season."* There is only one word that describes the manner of our preaching. "Be urgent." Manner is just as important as Matter, yea I dare say it is *more* important for communication than *what* we said.

What caused the council to marvel? Not *what* Peter and John said; they had heard that before several times, throughout Jerusalem, but they marvelled because of *how* they said it—at their "boldness." Soldiers came back empty-handed and reported not one word of *what* Jesus said, but *how* He said it. "Never a man *so spake*," they said in answer to the question, "Where is your prisoner?" When our Savior finished His Sermon on the Mount, the common folk were astonished, because He spoke with authority, and there was as much authority in His voice and face and manner as in His words. Anyone can tell when you are urgent, and when you are not!

A preacher said to me, "If you had the people in your audience to whom I speak, you would know why I lack enthusiasm." When there are those who agree with you and shout (maybe under their breath) "Amen! Preach it, brother!" and I want to remind you that there are always such "in season saints" present, you can't let them down. You won't disappoint them, will you? Your own mother is present with that special light in her eyes as she hears her son speak; you will give her all you have by way of eagerness, won't you? If your mother isn't there, there are many other mothers present, and they all, or many of them, are eager to hear. The time is always right. It is always "in season" for some people. If that is so, it should always be "in season" for you. Be urgent!!

B. *Be urgent "out of season."* Our Lord spoke to those "out of season" people in Revelation 3; "Behold," He said, "I keep on standing and keep on knocking. If anyone will answer my voice, I'll come in and live with him."

The folks in Laodicea didn't want to hear. It was "out of season," but our Lord kept right on insisting, right on calling. He was urgent.

It was surely "out of season" when Felix called Paul from his prison cell to give a little devotion before the judge and his wife. *How* did Paul speak? Take a look at Felix and Drucilla; he is trembling and she is burning! Why? It was not only the message of judgment, righteousness and self-control, but the total earnestness by which he spoke. "Go thy way, "Felix cried. But before Paul went back to prison, the Word had found its way into the heart of the hearer, because "out of season," God's preacher was urgent in pressing the claims of our Lord. There are always some Felix and Drucillas in every audience, whether they will hear, or will not hear. "Ye stiff necked and uncircumcised in heart and ears—ye do always resist the Holy Spirit. As your fathers did, so do ye. Ye who received the law through angels, which of the prophets did not your fathers betray and kill when they told before of the coming of the righteous One of whom ye have become betrayers and murderers!!" Stephen was urgent out of season, and he didn't need to sing an invitation song to get a response!

III. *How shall we develop our message when we preach the word?*

". . . reprove, rebuke, exhort, with all longsuffering and teaching," (II Tim. 4:2b).

A. *Prove it!* "Reprove"—"bring to the proof." Prove it, and then reprove it. There are *seven* forms of verbal support for any portion of the Word you preach.

1. You can explain, or use explanation like our Lord did to Nicodemus. "Except a man be born from above, be born of the water and the Spirit, he cannot see or enter into the Kingdom. That which is born of flesh is flesh; that which is born of Spirit is Spirit. Marvel not that I tell you that you *must* be born again," John 3:1-5ff. This is one of the most popular forms of proving a point, and it gets usually the same results our Lord got with Nicodemus; folks fail to listen or understand, (i.e., usually when you explain a truth).

2. You can use a parable (without such our Lord spake not unto them) i.e., He supported His points most effectively with an illustration either factual or hypothetical: "A certain man had two sons," "a certain man went down from

167

Jerusalem to Jericho," "the kingdom of heaven is like ten virgins." If you want to prove it and reprove it, and establish it, there is nothing like a good story. Franklin Delano Roosevelt was one of our most effective speakers. In seven short speeches he told 120 stories. Abraham Lincoln would have told 220 stories in the same number of speeches. How many windows do you have in your sermon as you preach the Word?

3. Prove it and reprove it by analogy and comparison. Stephen did it, and he really proved his point! The nations of Israel and their leaders in their treatment of the prophets were just like the present nation and their leaders in their treatment of Jesus their Messiah! Point by point the analogy and comparison came across with an irresistible conclusion.

4. Prove it and reprove it by specific instances, i.e., by undeveloped examples. Our Lord proved and demonstrated the nature of His role in the hearts of men by such a verbal support. He said: (a) The Kingdom of heaven is like a mustard seed—small, but powerful, (b) like leaven that permeates all it touches, (c) a treasure hidden and discovered in the ordinary field of life, (d) finding the rule of our Lord in our hearts is like finding one pearl of incalculable value, for which we sell all to obtain.

5. Prove it by personification. We hear people speak in the verbal supports of our Lord. His apostles learned to do the same thing; more

than half of the New Testament is narration: The prodigal son said, "Father, give me that portion of your substance that falleth unto me." Hundreds of pages in the Old Testament are narration. Real people live and speak in the Bible. If we do not hear and see and taste and touch *people*, we are not reproving as we should.

6. *Statistics* can be such a convincing form of proof. The whole Bible is a book of numbers and its message is confirmed by such verbal support. There are 14 generations from Abraham to David, and 14 generations from David to the exile in Babylon. People, thousands of them, went out from Jerusalem, all Judea, the whole region of the Jordan, confessing their sins as they heard John preach: If someone forces you to go *one* mile, go with him *two* miles. Look at the birds of the heavens (how many are there?). Who, by worrying can add a *single cubit* (18 inches) to his height? Large crowds (thousands) followed Him. I am a man under authority with soldiers under me (100 of them). When evening came *many* who were demon possessed (hundreds of them) were brought to Him, and He drove out the Spirits with a word and healed *all* the sick. "Foxes (how many?) have holes, and birds (how many?) have nests. *Two* demon possessed men who had a *legion* in them. A *large herd* of pigs (how many?) 2,000—we all know how many because Matthew and Mark used statistics to support

their point. Even the mention of a tax collector conjured up statistics or numbers in the minds of the hearers. The woman who had female trouble had it how long? *Twelve* years; we all know because of statistics. A *plentiful* harvest but *few* laborers. And He called *twelve* disciples to Him; these *twelve* Jesus sent out. Are not *two* sparrows sold for a *penny*? Yet not *one* of them will fall to the ground apart from the will of your Father. Even the hairs of your head are all numbered. So do not be afraid—you're worth more than many sparrows."

7. *Restatement* is a large part of the preaching of our Lord, John the Baptist, Paul, Peter; how many times did our Lord speak on money, on sex, on love, on faith? How often did John preach repentance? How repeatedly Peter preached that Jesus was the Christ! Repetition is not monotonous; preachers are! Restatement is one of the very best forms of verbal support.

B. *Apply it*! It should go without saying that the verbal supports discussed above are also related to applying the message; after all, the application will be verbally in some form. The point being made here is: Paul is saying unless we "rebuke" in our preaching, we have not preached the Word as he instructed us to. If the message we preach does not find specific relevance in the hearts of those who hear us, we are not preaching the Word. Let's take a look at the two grand examples of those who rebuked or related to their audience in their preaching:

"Ye men of Israel, hear these words: for these men are not drunk as ye suppose, seeing it is but the third hour of the day." (Peter verbally supports the rebuke element by explanation.) "But this is that which has been spoken by the prophet Joel"; (He now supports by analogy and comparison.). "And it shall be in the last days, saith God, I will pour forth my Spirit upon all flesh: And your sons and your daughters will prophesy, And your young men shall see visions, And your old men shall dream dreams: Yea and on my servants and on my hand-maidens in those days will I pour forth of my Spirit; and they shall prophesy. And I will show wonders in the heaven above, And signs on the earth beneath; Blood, fire, and vapor of smoke: The sun shall be turned into darkness, and the moon into blood, Before the day of the Lord comes, that great and notable day: And it shall be, that whosoever shall call on the name of the Lord shall be saved," (Acts 2:14-21).

We could extend the sermon to include all the verses in Acts, suffice it to say here that in verses 22 through 36, several forms of verbal support are used as Peter applies the message to such an extent that the audience cries out: "What shall we do?"

The second example is that of Paul as he spoke to the Athenians on Mars Hill: "Men of Athens! I see that in every way you are very religious." (Here he will support his point with specific instances.) We believe Luke has only given us the briefest of an outline of what Paul said. It is quite possible

171

that Paul mentioned briefly several objects of worship, "For as I walked around and observed your objects of worship, I even found an altar with this inscription: To An Unknown God. *Now what you worship as something unknown I am going to proclaim to you.*" (This is Paul's proposition in his message.) Luke gives us but the outline which is as follows:

I. Creator of all. 24-26.
1. Made all things.
2. Lord of heaven and earth.
3. Dwells not in any one place.
4. Not served by men's hands.
5. The maker of nations.

II. Within the reach of all. 27-29.
1. In Him we live, move and have our being.
2. We are His offspring or creation.
3. Cast away then these idols and worship the true God.

III. Gives salvation to all. 30-31.
1. The days of ignorance are over.
2. Men now should repent and turn to Christ.
3. This to be done in lieu of the final judgment.

What we are saying here is: unless the message finds fulfillment in the ears of the listener, it is not preaching of the Word as our Lord did it (cf. Luke 4:14-21).

C. *Exhort*—This is the action word; all our sermons must contain the call for response. Once again we say that the seven forms of verbal support will be used in developing "exhort," even as with reprove and rebuke. However, there is an added element

172

here. We must add a motive appeal. There must be some reason for acting! We could prove a point, apply it, and then we must offer some purpose for acting upon what has been said. As a very simple example: I could prove there is a hell; I could demonstrate that you are going there, but the motive of *fear* must be included in the exhortation to escape it. Or, perhaps the motive of *gratitude* that our Savior died to save you from such a place.

This discussion might appear a bit involved for some of you. To put the matter very simply; we believe Paul expects each of these elements in every message. Somewhere in every sermon there is a point to be proved, a point to be applied, and a point upon which we must and will act. The total impact of our whole sermon is that we have proven it, applied it and called for action upon it.

Read the eight sermons in the New Testament and discover the obvious use of these three essential elements in each one of them.

D. *Such preaching must be done with great patience and careful instruction.* The listeners place more importance on what you are than what you say. If you are impatient and censorious, if you are hard and cruel in your attitude, it will be communicated and all the audience hears will be sifted through an almost impenetrable barrier. On the other hand, if they see the very love of God in your demeanor, tears of concern upon your cheeks —if they hear you explain, illustrate, apply, time

173

after time after time, with longsuffering kindness, they will believe what you say. Your manner speaks more eloquently than your mouth. In the above concern with loving patience, we must not forget the "careful instruction" necessary to the solid content of what we, with great patience, present. In this point, we have used the verbal support. It would be so much clearer and more convincing if we were to cite five or six specific instances, or if we personified a situation where we could hear the point instead of having it explained. It would be easy to relate examples from the life of our Lord: (1) Washing the apostle's feet, John 13:1-13; (2) His words to the sleeping apostles in the garden, (3) His patience in teaching the meaning of the parables; (4) His dying words on the cross.

IV. *Why should we preach the word?* (vs. 3, 4).

"For the time will come when they will not endure the sound doctrine; but, having itching ears, will heap to themselves teachers after their own lusts; and will turn away their ears from the truth, and turn aside unto fables, (II Tim. 4:3, 4).

A. Because the time is coming, (yea, now is) when men will not want to hear it. Paul is evidently talking about religious people, because he speaks in the next verse of teachers of some competitive doctrine. America today is so much like the nation of Israel in their declining days just before their captivity:

174

1. *Isaiah* - preached God's word on idolatry to idolators; they would have none of it!
2. *Jeremiah* - preached God's word to the materially secure; they would not hear him!
3. *Ezekiel* - preached the word about adultery and sexual sin; "away! away! We want none of it!"

We have committed a double sin; we seldom seek to speak to those who are involved in the destruction of our nation and when we do, we fail to call them to repentance.

B. We need to preach the word because there are competitors—those who speak what men want to hear.

1. "What is wrong with working three jobs? A man has to pay his bills." That's not your problem; you are paying homage to your idol of the lust of the eyes. You can offer all the rationale you want to justify American Materialism, and we hear much of it. But God still says real life does not consist in the American way of living, which is to a very large extent the abundance of things that a man has.
2. "Jesus never condemned riches; it is because of God's goodness that we have all of our material wealth." "We should enjoy what God has given us"; If we think past the obvious we can see the lies in such statements. Jesus died to condemn some rich men—the hypocritically rich Pharisees of his day who excused their covetousness by hiding behind the tax dodge of the temple.

175

"We would really like to help, but we have all our money in the Temple service." Of course, they never told you and you were not supposed to know, who controlled that sacked "corbin" currency. The fact that men have much proves nothing, i.e., by itself. Consider Nebuchadnezzar, or Nero, or Pharaoh.

3. Because man will turn aside from truth to myths, this temptation rears its attractive head. This is a flat lie out of the mind of Satan! Lust is in the heart before it uses the eyes; if you are pure in heart, you will see God everywhere and on every occasion. Such purity begins with a commitment and continues through discipline. How is it that some preachers are always involved in this temptation and others are not? Because one preacher was looking for it and the other was not. Commit yourself to one woman and buffet your body; you will be calm, cool and steady in your service of preaching the Word.

V. *What should be our constant purpose in preaching the word?* (vs. 5).

"But be thou sober in all things, suffer hardship, do the work of an evangelist, fulfill thy ministry" (II Tim. 4:5).

A. To be always balanced in our preaching. The word "sober" carries with it the thought of not being drunk; not from alcohol or liquor, but from other far stronger intoxicants always available to the preacher:

176

1. The strong drink of false pride. There are always a few silly women who will compliment you on anything and everything you say. There are times when you have said something as well as anyone has said it. Wait a moment before you congratulate yourself. Who congratulated our Lord after His Sermon on the Mount? They were astonished, they were impressed, but no one said "what a message!" and from the reaction in the lives of His disciples, most of them were not converts.

   What was the response to His message on the *bread from heaven*? They went home! How fragile was our Lord's ego? He neither congratulated himself nor became discouraged at the lack of response or understanding, because He was proud of His Father and His work, and not of Himself and His preaching.

2. The strong drink of party pressure. When Jesus became popular, everyone hoped He would join their group or party. Our Lord was not a Pharisee, but He did believe in the Spirit world, in the resurrection and in angels, but He let them know in no uncertain terms that they were woefully short in several areas. Our Lord was not a Sadducee but He did agree with them on some points, especially as they disagreed with the Pharisee's traditions.

   The preacher is under constant pressure to drink from someone's well, either in the local pressure groups, in the community or in the brotherhood and in the denominational world.

177

You can tell when a man speaks whether he is drunk or not. Many preachers give obvious evidence from their speaking that they have been imbibing at the bar of thinking more highly of themselves than they ought, or they have stopped for a long draught at the bottle of party pride, or perhaps it is from the terrible brew of the lust of the flesh; your speech will betray you—beware!

It can also be easily detected that the preacher has been often drinking at the well of life served by our Lord and backed by His promise that He who keeps on drinking here will always see things through the eyes of God.

B. To be always *disciplined*. I need not mention that the oft used word "suffer hardship" is related to the area of self-control. It was used frequently of the soldier and the self-imposed rigors of army life. Self-control in the use of words is perhaps the most difficult of all. All discipline begins in the mind; if we do not control our thoughts we will ultimately control nothing. When every thought is captive to our wonderful Lord, the words of our mouth will indeed be just what He would want.

C. To be always evangelistic. The work of an evangelist is to preach to the lost with the good news. We can do many other tasks, and some of them are quite acceptable and profitable to the work of our Lord, but if we do not talk to the lost about their need, we leave not done the work of an evangelist. Philip served the Lord as he served tables,

178

but he also preached to the lost in Samaria and on the way to Gaza. Peter and the eleven were called to be trained by Jesus and filled with the Holy Spirit, but they spoke to the lost on Pentecost. Evangelism begins and ends with an attitude. We are the light of the world, not the light of the church. We are the salt of the earth, not the salt of the body of Christ. We are sent to the lost first, last and always.

D. To always "fill up" your service or ministry. It is not at all difficult to be always busy, but it is very difficult to be filled up with service for our Lord. Our Lord's purpose was seeking and saving the lost. His eternally important purpose was ever before Him. Everywhere with everyone He pursued His goal; His seeking and saving cost Him His life, and so it will with us. When we fill up our lives in a concern for the lost, we will have fulfilled our ministry.

Conclusion:

It is my deepest concern that each of you be able to answer these six questions:

1. What is the Word we preach?
   Answer: The Bible.
2. Who is in our audience?
   Answer: God, the author of the Word,
   Jesus, the coming Judge,
   The citizens of King Jesus' Kingdom.
3. How and When is the best time to preach?
   Answer: Urgently in season; urgently out of season.

179

4. How shall we develop the message?
   Answer: Prove it, apply it, call for action on it.

5. Why should we preach the Word?
   Answer: Some do not want to know,
   There are competitors.

6. What should be our constant purpose in preaching the Word?
   Answer: To be always balanced, disciplined, evangelistic, and fulfilling in our preaching.

BIOGRAPHICAL SKETCHES
OF THE AUTHORS

Don DeWelt

Don DeWelt is a professor at Ozark Bible College in Joplin, Missouri, where he has taught homiletics, Acts, expository preaching, and personal evangelism. He also holds special seminars on the Holy Spirit and developing personal worship. Mr. DeWelt has been preaching and teaching the Word for 46 years. He is a preacher and teacher and author. At the present time he is editor and president of College Press Publishing Company.

Douglas A. Dickey

Douglas A. Dickey was born in Indiana. He attended Butler University, Howard University, Purdue University and California State University.

Mr. Dickey ministered at Williamsport Christian Church from 1938 to 1966. He served as army chaplain from 1944 to 1946 and was campus minister at Purdue University from 1966 to 1982. He now is campus minister at California State University in Fullerton and also teaches at Pacific Christian College.

Mr. Dickey has written four books: *Questions Teens Ask About Religion, Sermons for Sidetracked Saints, The Word of Life* and *What Else.*

Charles R. Gresham

Charles R. Gresham is professor of the Bible and Christian Education at Kentucky Christian College, Grayson, Kentucky. He has studied at Manhattan Bible College, Phillips University Seminary, Perkins School of Theology,

Southern Methodist University, Southwestern Baptist Theological Seminary, Central State College, and Kansas State University. Dr. Gresham received a Doctor's Degree in Religious Education from Southwestern Baptist Theological Seminary. Dr. Gresham has been a minister of several churches, lecturer, author, seminar leader, evangelist, editor, and professor at several Christian colleges. He has a strong belief in preaching expository sermons to the lost of this world.

Edwin V. Hayden

Edwin V. Hayden attended Roanoke College at Salem, Butler School of Religion, Butler University, Kentucky Christian College and Milligan College.

Dr. Hayden began preaching in 1934. After over two decades of instilling the Word of God in the hearts and minds of the people with whom he served, Dr. Hayden taught for five years (1952-57) at Ozark Bible College. There he conveyed to a generation of students something of his enthusiasm for Biblical studies, Christian journalism, and expository preaching.

In 1957 Dr. Hayden became editor of *Christian Standard*. Among his first projects as editor was the development of an essay series on expository preaching. After twenty years he retired from the editorship.

Currently he teaches a class in expository preaching at the Cincinnati Christian Seminary. His latest publication *Preaching Through the Bible* from College Press Publishing Company is an excellent example of his expository preaching expertise and application.

182

E. Ray Jones

E. Ray Jones received his education at Cincinnati Bible Seminary and the University of Kentucky. He also taught practical ministries at Cincinnati Bible Seminary and other colleges. He served as the minister for twelve years at Gardenside Christian Church in Lexington, Kentucky. He ministered at East 38th Street Christian Church in Indianapolis, Indiana, for ten years. His present ministry is at the First Christian Church of Clearwater, Florida, where he has served for nine years. While at Clearwater he also helped established the Tarpon Springs Church.

Mr. Jones has been the president of the North American Christian Convention in 1975-76. He has preached in Africa Middle East, Europe, Australia, and New Zealand. He is an author of many lessons and articles for the *Christian Standard* and the author of *Sermon for the Space Age*. Mr. Jones stands as God's man who preaches the Word to the world.

Marshall J. Leggett

Marshall J. Leggett, president of Milligan College, Milligan, Tennessee, has faithfully served as a minister of the gospel for 35 years. Dr. Leggett has received his B.A. cum laude (Milligan); M.Div. with honors (Christian Theological Seminary); Doctor of Divinity (Milligan); Doctor of Sacred Letters (Midwest Christian College). He has served in several churches in Tennessee, Ohio, Indiana and Kentucky and has served the brotherhood in various aspects especially with the NACC as both president (1971) and vice president (1965) and on numerous occasions has been a part of various NACC committees. He has also been involved as a trustee of two schools and serves on several different boards for Christian organizations. Dr. Leggett was born Dec. 6, 1929 in Washington, North Carolina.

Wilford Franklin Lown

Wilford Franklin Lown was born and raised in Iowa. He attended Manhattan Christian College, Kansas State University, Kentucky Christian College, and Milligan College.

Dr. Lown has ministered in churches in Arkansas, Wisconsin, Missouri and Kansas. He now serves as senior minister of Central Christian Church of Wichita, Kansas. He served as president of Manhattan Christian College from 1955 to 1981. He was president of the North American Christian Convention in 1973.

Dr. Lown is the author of three books, *Prayer Thought, The Restoration Movement and Its Meaning for Today,* and *They Shall Run and Not Be Weary.* He has also written numerous articles for religious periodicals.

Orval M. Morgan

Orval M. Morgan has been a minister of the gospel for over 61 years. He was born and grew to manhood in Indiana. He attended Cincinnati Bible Seminary and Butler University and has ministered in Indiana, Iowa, Illinois and Kentucky.

An outstanding emphasis of Dr. Morgan's life has been his enthusiasm for preaching. He served as head of the

Department of Evangelism and Christian Ministries at Midwest Christian College in Oklahoma City. Even though he is now retired he still preaches, lectures and holds evangelistic meetings. Dr. Morgan's ministries can be characterized as evangelistic and centered on church growth.

Don H. Sharp

Don H. Sharp has been preaching for many years. He has ministered in churches in Virginia, West Virginia, Tennessee, Indiana, Kentucky, and Illinois. As an evangelist he has served for six years. As a writer he has written for *Restoration Herald* and *Christian Standard*. He wrote two books *Forty Six Sharp Points* and *The Obidian Frog*. He also wrote two children's programs *Bird in a Box* and *Animals in an Ark*. As a teacher he has taught a seminar on hospital calling at Lincoln Christian College and is a field education superior at Christian Theological Seminary.

At present Mr. Sharp is serving as minister of the newly organized Maranatha Christian Church, Kokomo, Indiana. He is also director of the Creative Pastoral Resources of Greentown, Indiana. Mr. Sharp has given himself to serving Christ and preaching God's Word.

Knofel Staton

Knofel Staton attended Lincoln Christian College, Illinois State University, Indiana University, Southwestern Baptist Theological Seminary, Kentucky State, Wheaton Graduate School of Theology, and University of Iowa. He has ministered and served in churches in Illinois, Indiana,

Iowa, Missouri, and California. He is an author of over twenty books. He taught at Ozark Bible College in Joplin, Missouri, expository preaching, New Testament Church, I Corinthians, and many other topics. He is at present the president of Pacific Christian College in Fullerton, California, and also teaches. Mr. Staton is truly a man of God who preaches and teaches God's Word.

Sam E. Stone

Sam E. Stone was born in New Mexico. He attended Ozark Bible College, Cincinnati Bible Seminary, Earlham College, University of Missouri, and Kentucky Christian College.

He has served in churches in Missouri and Ohio. He taught journalism courses at Cincinnati Bible College and Central Christian College. He continues as guest lecturer in practical ministry and journalism at the Cincinnati Bible Seminary. He edited *Straight* magazine in 1958 to 1960 and is presently editor of *Christian Standard*. He has written numerous articles in relgious periodicals. He also is author of two books, *Grounded Faith for Growing Christians* and *The Christian Minister*.